CAN MY
BRIDESMAIDS
WEAR
BLACK?

Marjabelle Young Stewart

CAN MY BRIDESMAIDS WEAR

BLACK?

*. . . and 325 Other Most-Asked
Etiquette Questions*

ST. MARTIN'S PRESS • New York

DESIGN BY JUDITH A. STAGNITTO

Library of Congress Cataloging-in-Publication Data

Stewart, Marjabelle Young.
    Can my bridesmaids wear black?— and 325 other most-asked
etiquette questions / Marjabelle Young Stewart.
        p. cm.
    ISBN 0-312-03300-1
    1. Etiquette—United States—Miscellanea. I. Title.
BJ1853.S873 1989
395—dc20   89-30430
                                                           CIP

First Edition
10 9 8 7 6 5 4 3 2

Dedicated to my beautiful family: husband, Bill; daughter, Jacqueline; son, Bill, Jr.; and the apple of my eye, Erin Marjabelle, my granddaughter.

·CONTENTS·

Acknowledgments   *ix*

Introduction   *xi*

1. Getting Along with Family and Friends   *1*

2. Community Life   *20*

3. Your Business Life   *28*

4. Your Public Performances   *44*

5. Entertaining and Being Entertained   *55*

6. The Art of Giving and Receiving   *70*

7. Written Communication 77

8. Ceremonies and Celebrations 99

9. Weddings 115

10. Personal Loss 140

11. Tipping 162

·ACKNOWLEDGMENTS·

My deep appreciation to Marian Faux for her exper-
tise and care in completing the manuscript. To my
editor Barbara Anderson, for her thoroughness, and
to assistant editor Anne Savarese, for always being
there when I need her. And warmest thanks to my
agent, Dominick Abel.

· INTRODUCTION ·

OVER THE YEARS, an enormous quantity of mail has found its way to my doorstep, some of it addressed only to *Etiquette Lady, Kewanee, Illinois.* Recently, as I was going through my very large correspondence file, with an eye for throwing it away, it dawned on me that there was something else I might better do with it: I would share it with you. On the cusp of that idea, this small book was born, as a gift to you, my readers.

I thought the letters were worth sharing because of what they revealed about us. I saw that there were patterns to the kinds of questions you asked and even that you tended to ask the same questions over and over. It also did not escape my notice that you frequently asked questions on behalf of others—sisters, sisters-in-law, neighbors, parents, children, and so on. In this sense, this book of my letters takes on the aura of an advice column, where I am, I hope, an objective bystander who can help to smooth the wrinkles out of everyday living.

Each of us lives in several different worlds, and it is these worlds that I have chosen to use as divisions for this book. We live in the worlds of our family and friends, in our communities, in our business worlds, and so on.

And of course, since we are all human, we deal with the same kinds of basic life problems. A daughter is getting married, and we want to ensure that she has a wonderful—and wonderfully proper—wedding. We are trimming a Christmas-card list and need to know how to do it in the most tactful way. We are undergoing a divorce and need to know how to handle the public—and the private—side of this trauma.

I have read that a cook is contented if she can harvest only one good recipe from a cookbook. I shall be content if between the covers of this book you find a few more—but not necessarily many more—letters that help you see your way through a puzzling situation.

In closing, I want to leave you with one word of caution, a message that is at the center of all my books. Even though these letters often give hard-and-fast rules or very concrete suggestions for what to do in certain situations, there is not necessarily a rule to cover every situation, a right and wrong way of doing everything. Manners are really about treating others as we ourselves would like to be treated: with love and consideration.

MARJABELLE STEWART
June 1989

CAN MY BRIDESMAIDS WEAR

BLACK?

1

GETTING ALONG
WITH FAMILY
AND FRIENDS

·Family Relationships·

Q Two sisters in my family—they're my cousins—maintain a long-standing feud and will not attend the same party. Each insists that the other one not be invited. I'm having a big party this summer for the entire family and am unsure how to handle them. Should I invite them both and tell them? Invite them both and not tell them? I'd rather not get personally involved in this quarrel.
A You shouldn't get involved. Send invitations to both sisters and let them work it out. If either sister calls and threatens not to attend, tell her the decision is entirely hers to make.

Q I'm not sure how to introduce my various step-relatives. Can you give me any advice?
A I know a young woman who introduces her stepgrandmother as her grandmother. She says the older woman is the only grandmother she has ever known on her mother's side of

the family. When people comment on the (nonexistent) family resemblance, she accepts the compliment with a big smile and a "Thank you."

While this is one way to handle this situation when a stepparent (or grandparent) has replaced a natural parent, it is not the only solution, and it can lead to confusion in today's extended families where everyone is alive and kicking. In this situation it would be misleading—and uncomfortable—for most persons to introduce a step-relative as a natural parent. Nothing is wrong with using the word "step" when introducing someone. Simply say, "I'd like you to meet my stepmother, Jane Smith."

Q I have two sets of parents (natural and step) and one half brother as well as two stepsisters. How do I introduce everyone? **A** No bad connotations should be attached to introducing them as what they are: your half brother or your stepsisters. To do otherwise may only lead to further questions and confusion.

Q I'm not sure what to call my in-laws, and they haven't said anything about this in the six months that I've been married. **A** Years ago, in-laws were called "Mother-in-law" and "Father-in-law," but this seems unnecessarily stiff today. On the other hand, most of us seem to have trouble calling someone other than our own parents "Mother" and "Father."

An informal poll of my friends and acquaintances reveals that most sons- and daughters-in-law use first names for their in-laws—or they don't call them anything, at least until they have children. After that they call them "Grandmother" and "Grandfather," which is still awkward in these days of youthful grandparents. Some of my older friends resisted being called by their first names but still thought it was better than being called nothing.

It is basically up to the older person to indicate to a younger person what he or she wishes to be called. But judging from the number of letters I get about this subject, I think parents are reluctant to settle this question. Why don't you open the discussion with your parents-in-law? Begin by asking them what they would like to be called. If they suggest something that makes you uncomfortable, tell them why you would not be comfortable calling them this. Ask if they would mind if you called them something else, and offer your suggestion.

Q   My brother-in-law is a bigot and, of course, he thinks I'm a raving liberal even though I'm actually rather middle-of-the-road. He seems to delight in telling sexist and racist jokes in my presence. What can I do to let him know how uncomfortable I am with this kind of humor?

A   First, don't rise to the bait. While it is kind to laugh at a bad joke or a good joke badly told, no one is obligated to perpetuate jokes that are designed to denigrate others. Pretend you didn't hear the joke or refuse to respond to it in any way. If you can do so without seeming too abrupt, walk away when he starts to tell such jokes.

Q   When I have a dinner party, am I obligated to invite my or my husband's siblings?

A   You are not obliged to invite them to every party, nor should they expect that you will. Close relatives are usually invited to big parties—the holiday open house, for example, or a housewarming.

Q   We have a family gift exchange every Christmas at a big party with everyone present. One of my sisters-in-law sends thank-you notes. She has let me know that she thinks I'm remiss for not sending them, too. I don't think they're necessary. What is the proper etiquette on this?

A   Thank-you notes are unnecessary if you were all present and thanked one another when you opened the gifts. It is a nice touch to call a day or so after the gift exchange to thank people again for their presents. And of course, if you receive any gifts from people who are not present, they deserve a thank-you note and/or a phone call.

As for your sister-in-law, thank her for her notes, but don't feel pressured by them.

Q My mother-in-law, after five years of knowing me, always gives me totally inappropriate clothing as a gift. She chooses unflattering colors and styles. She always tells me to return these gifts if I don't like them, but we see each other so often that I'm afraid I'll offend her. I tend to wear the things she gives once or twice in her presence, and then they hang forever in my closet. What do you suggest?

A Your mother-in-law may be one of those persons who can't buy things that aren't to her taste—and she's trying to dress you, I'll bet, the way she herself dresses. But there are several possible solutions.

First, take her at her word when she says you should return the clothes. If you return enough of them, maybe she'll get the hint and either stop buying you clothes or pay attention to your taste.

Second, enlist your husband's support. Try on your mother-in-law's presents in front of him, and let him say what is wrong with them. He can say, "Gee, Mom, I don't think that shade of green is June's color" or "I'm not sure I like pleated skirts on you, honey." It's a gentle way of getting the message across.

If all else fails, you might tactfully explain the situation to her. Begin by telling her how grateful you are for her attempts to buy you clothes, and go on to say that you are difficult to fit or that you need to see a color on you to know whether it's truly right for you, and that perhaps you should shop for your own clothes. She may stop buying you clothes, but I can't promise that she'll stop buying you gifts that aren't to your taste.

Q My family (sisters and brothers) has always exchanged Christmas presents, but as we have all had children, I now find that I'm obligated to buy more presents than my husband and I can afford—sixteen in all just for my family alone. I don't want to seem cheap, buy I don't know how many more Christmases I can shoulder this burden. Any suggestions?

A At some point, for the very reason you suggest—the family gets too large—most families reorganize their gift giving at Christmas. Don't hesitate to suggest doing this. I can promise you that you aren't the only family member feeling the pinch. Here are some money-saving suggestions:

- Organize a grab bag rather than giving individual presents.
- Buy gifts for the children only and dispense with gifts for the adults.
- Buy a joint gift for your parents. Most elderly persons have all the small household presents they will ever need and would welcome a larger gift, such as a television or back-yard grill, that they might not buy themselves. By banding together, you children can buy nicer presents than you might individually—and spend less doing it.
- Set a price limit on gifts. I know one family that gives each other wonderfully creative and often handmade pre-sents—and they have a $5 limit per gift.

Q I'm a thirty-year-old woman with a very embarrassing prob-lem. I want to be able to sleep with the man I live with when I visit my parents. My parents know we live together and have never expressed their approval or disapproval. When they visit us, they stay in a hotel because we don't have room for them. When we visit them, they put us in separate bedrooms. I'm not exactly a teenager, so I think my request is reasonable. What's the best way to handle this problem?

A I would agree that a thirty-year-old is old enough to sleep with whomever she pleases. Since your parents have never expressed disapproval over your living arrangements, it will be worthwhile to explore this issue with them. Before you visit, tell them you would like to share a bedroom with your lover.

If they disapprove, you have two choices: Stay with them in their house and abide by their wishes or visit them and stay in a hotel or motel. Whatever you decide to do, do it amicably. Don't sulk over your parents' decision.

Q Holidays are a crazy time for my husband and our three children. Even though we have to drive 100 miles to get to my parents' house, and another 40 miles to my husband's parents' house, we always visit both sets of parents on every major holiday, and it's a madhouse. The kids end up exhausted, and we end up ready to drown them. We realize we can't keep up this double duty, but we don't know a gracious way out. What do you suggest?

A Many people try to divide every holiday among two families, when I think the more pleasant situation all around is to divvy up the holidays themselves. Spend one Christmas with one family one year and the other family the next year. Or go to one family for Passover one year and another the following year.

Alternatively, consider spending a holiday at home occasionally and visiting your parents at some other time of the year. I know families think they should be together for holidays, and they should—but for some, not necessarily all, holidays. Many couples use their children as a very legitimate reason to stay home at Christmas and visit their parents at a less hectic time of year.

If you want to be gracious about this, give each set of parents a choice (on alternate years) of which holidays they would like you present for.

Q I have an unusual situation. My husband and I visit my parents, who live 500 miles away, every autumn and spring for about a week. Our problem is this: My parents have begun to live an increasingly sedentary life as they've gotten older, and we find ourselves bored after a couple of days. We've asked them to do things with us—go to movies, out to dinner—but they're not interested. It's not practical to go for a shorter visit, and I do love them and want to visit them. Can you suggest anything to help?

A Your situation is not so unusual. Many people who love seeing their parents (or anyone else) find that long visits wear a little thin after the first few days. Or one's parents may not have many interests in common with one's spouse. The solution: Go off by yourselves for a while. Your instincts to include your parents in your invitations are gracious, but if they aren't interested in going to a movie or out to dinner, that doesn't rule out these activities for you.

One young couple I know who live in Manhattan and visit her parents in Indiana have found that these visits provide them with an excellent opportunity to indulge in something they can't do in Manhattan: They go hiking in the state parks near her parents' house.

Q When my boyfriend and I visit my parents for a few days, we always find that they expect us to settle in to their schedule rather than making an attempt to ask us about ours. For example, they eat dinner at six o'clock sharp, while we like to eat dinner later. Do you think we could suggest eating dinner a little later?

A When you are a guest in someone's home (even your own parents'), you are expected to pick up on and follow their routines rather than the other way around. There are other, less obvious, ways you can break the routine that makes you uncomfortable. The two of you can plan to go out to dinner or a movie or perhaps to visit some old friends. You parents will undoubtedly welcome the break from nonstop entertaining as much as

you will welcome the chance to do something on your own
schedule.

· Friendships ·

Q My husband and I met a couple we like very much at another friend's house over dinner. Where do we go from here in
initiating the friendship?

A Anytime you meet someone socially (and often in a business
context as well) whom you would like to know better, you may
take the initiative in arranging to see each other again. When
you meet someone through a friend, though, it is polite to invite
the person or couple who initially brought you together the first
time you see your new friends.

Q We met some people at a party who would very much like
to become friends with us, but I'm afraid my husband and I
aren't interested in pursuing this. They have asked us to dinner
and to a party. We went to dinner and declined the party
invitation. Must I invite them back? Any ideas on how we can
cool this friendship?

A When you know you don't wish to pursue a relationship, the
kindest thing to do is to turn down all invitations from the start.
Since you accepted one, you owe a return invitation. How about
including this couple in a big party or open house you are giving?
One way to send the message that you aren't very interested is
to let several months elapse between invitations.

Q A friend has done something I find unforgivable, and I want
to end the friendship. I'm not sure she knows this, however.
What should I do?

A No matter what has happened, I think you owe your friend
an explanation. Call her to talk or, if you find this too difficult,

drop her a note explaining why you are offended. If you truly feel you cannot continue the relationship, tell her this, too. But do try to heal the wound if at all possible. Friendship is too precious to throw away if it can possibly be saved.

Q What can you do when someone asks you a personal question you would rather not answer?
A Such questions are rude, although they are sometimes asked innocently by people who don't know any better. The most common such question is for someone to ask the price of something. You can usually say you don't remember. I sometimes pretend I didn't hear a personal question if I can do so without hurting the questioner's feelings. Alternatively, I try to change the subject.

If someone persists in asking a question, a good technique is to turn the tables on them and ask them why they want to know. Most people will back off at this point.

Considerate people don't ask questions about topics that might be touchy to the person who has to answer them. If you know someone is not working, for example, don't ask him or her why. Considerate people, in fact, avoid asking questions about the following topics:

- Age
- Surgery
- Serious illness in a family
- Therapy
- Politics
- Weight
- Personal loss
- Fertility
- Income
- Homosexuality
- Religion

- Race
- Disabilities
- Prices, including clothing, jewelry, and houses

Q I have a friend who loves to argue. He will start an argument anywhere and at any time, even at a party. How can I control him at a dinner party?

A Although some hostesses like a heated dinner-table discussion, most would prefer that their guests stick to noncontroversial topics. When confronted with someone who wants to argue, smile and say, "I guess we just have to agree to disagree about that" or "I'm sure we could have a fascinating conversation about that, but this really isn't the place to do so, is it?"

Q Our son tells us that friends of ours invited him to go to the circus several months ago when the subject came up in casual conversation, even though they have said nothing about this to us. I don't want him to be disappointed, but I'm afraid they may have forgotten the invitation. They have done other things with him, so I believe they did make the offer. Should I say something to them?

A I applaud your friends' efforts to befriend your child as well as you.

I agree with you that your child should not be disappointed—if in fact this is in your control. A woman I know who has been put in this situation said that she would call her friends and say, "Jake says you have invited him to the circus. He may have misunderstood your conversation, or if you did ask him, it may no longer be convenient for you to take him, but I just wanted to double-check with you." The virtue of this phrasing is that it gives your friends an out if they cannot keep the engagement (although invitations extended to children should be, if anything, less breakable than those to adults), and it reminds them that the event is coming up, if they do intend to fulfill their obligation.

Q My husband and I have struck up a friendship with an elderly man who lives in our apartment building. He asked us to brunch one day but we could not accept. We would like to invite him back but cannot imagine that he would fit in with our friends—or even that he would enjoy them, since they are about forty years younger than he is. What do you suggest?

A I think you are underestimating everyone's capacity here. We all need and enjoy friends of varying ages. You wouldn't want all your friends to share your occupation, so why should all your friends be the same age? Elderly people often welcome the opportunity to get together with younger persons, and your peers, if they are sophisticated and polite, should have no trouble enjoying the company of this elderly man.

Q At age eight, my daughter is now old enough to want to entertain her friends in our home. She has already been invited several times to spend the night with friends, but I have not let her go because the invitations came from her friend and not the friend's parents, whom I do not know in any event. We live in a big city, and I feel extra precautions are necessary. Can you give me any guidelines on this?

A I understand your fears, but I think you are being overly cautious about this. Parents of children who are friends have a reason to know one another, and it does not matter which one of you initiates the acquaintanceship. The next time your daughter comes home with an invitation to spend the night with a friend, call the friend's mother to confirm the invitation and so that you will know the mother before you send your child to her house.

It's important, I feel, to encourage your children to bring their friends home, although they should always check with you before extending an invitation. Very young children will not have learned this, however, and if your child says to you, in front of her friend, "Can Janie eat dinner with us tonight?" it is perfectly acceptable for you to say, "No, not tonight, because we didn't plan for her to do so and dinner will be waiting for her at her house. But you can ask her another night."

Q   I'm a single woman in my late twenties whose friendships seem to be in transition. The people I went to school with are scattered all over the country, and I only see some of my best friends once or twice a year. Some of my college friends who live nearby are married and seem to have no time for me—or maybe I'm the one who is uncomfortable around them. Besides, once they have children, they never have time for anything. Help! I need some new friends but don't know how to make them.

A   All of us go through transition periods when we need to make new friends, and the years after school are one of the first of several such periods in your life that you will encounter. While acknowledging that some friendships do not stand the test of time (our interests change and we no longer have so much in common, or we're at completely different stages in our lives), I urge you to hang on to your old friends at the same time you acquire new ones.

First, let's talk about hanging on to the old ones. Even though you say you feel uncomfortable with friends who have married and had children, try to maintain those friendships, although you may have to be the one who makes an attempt to be flexible, since your schedule will be less demanding than those of your friends who are parents. When friends move away, try to keep in touch by letter and telephone.

But you also need to make some new friends, and you're at a stage in your life where this should be relatively easy to do. You do need some new places to make them, though, since you no longer have a school setting to provide you with a social life. Here are some other places to look for friends:

- Work. It's the most obvious place, since you will doubtless share many interests with your colleagues.

- Church or temple. Join a young people's group or volunteer for a service program.
- Sports. If you enjoy a particular sport, make arrangements to play it or take a class. If you need a partner, sign up for a league or take a couple of lessons, and then ask your instructor to match you with someone of equal playing skills.
- Volunteer work. It's the most rewarding way to meet other people.
- Night school and hobby groups. Follow up on something that interests you, and you're sure to find kindred spirits.
- Alumnae or sorority or fraternal organizations. Even though you're no longer in school, some of the organizations that existed there will have local chapters where you will meet people with whom you will have something in common. Join your sorority's local alumnae group or your school's alumnae group.

· Introductions ·

Q   When I introduce my parents, do I call them "Mr. and Mrs. Jones" or use their first names?
A   Use the name they will use when talking with the person whom they are meeting. If you are introducing your father to one of your friends who will call him "Mr. Jones," then say, "Dad, I'd like you to meet Ron. Ron, this is my father, Mr. Jones."

If you are introducing your parent to a peer (someone his or her own age, for example), then say, "Mrs. Smith, I'd like you to meet my father, Sam Jones. Dad, this is Eileen Smith."

Q   Although I'm not comfortable with this, my twelve-year-old son's friends all call me by my first name. Will I look too stuffy if I correct them?

A No, it's your prerogative as the older person to be called whatever you choose. In many circles today, young people do call their parents' friends by their first names, but you may say, with a smile, "Timmy, I'd prefer that you called me Mrs. Ryan."

Parents should teach children to address their elders by "Mr." and "Mrs." until asked to do otherwise.

Q How should I introduce my ex-mother-in-law?

A If you are introducing her to a casual acquaintance or someone who will not pursue the relationship, there is no need to mention the association. Simply introduce her as "Mrs. (or Mary) Hindenberg."

There are occasions, of course, where you will want to clarify your former relationship. Do so as tactfully as possible, by saying, "This is Jack's mother" or, "I'd like you to meet Susie's grandmother."

Q It seems like everyone uses first names instantly these days. Is there ever a time when this is inappropriate?

A The use of first names has become pervasive in our society today, but there are still a few occasions when first names are best not used. These are:

- When meeting someone of higher rank. Obviously you would not call the president of the United States by his or her first name, and you also would not call any other high government official by his or her first name unless invited to do so.
- When meeting someone elderly. Older persons especially appreciate the courtesy of being called "Mr.," "Miss," or "Mrs."
- Doctors rendering personal services usually prefer to be called "Dr. Goodhealth." A physician should also refer to patients (except those he knows well or with whom he has

a personal relationship) by their last names, and if he calls you by your first name, I see no reason that you should not call him by his.

- Finally, depending upon the circumstances (meaning an individual's age and status), use titles and last names with superiors at work and clients until given a sign that first names are acceptable.

Q I know that everyone uses first names these days, but I don't like it when doormen and salespeople assume they can call me by my first name. How should I handle this?
A About the only thing I can suggest is that you introduce yourself to service personnel as "Mr. (or Mrs.) Goodwill." If they don't know your first name, it will be hard to call you by it. If they already call you by your first name, try a little persistence. When you identify yourself to them, always say you are Mr. or Mrs. Goodwill.

Q When introducing people, I get flustered and forget who should be introduced to whom. Can you give me any hints?
A Remember that one person is introduced to another, as in:
"Mother, I'd like you to meet Carol, my new roommate."
"Mr. Smith, this is Ronald, our temp worker for this week."
"Mary, may I introduce my husband, Bill."
"Mr. Mayor, may I present Samuel Riley."
Introduce the lower-ranking person to the higher-ranking person. Basically, this means:

- Introduce people to religious and government officials:
  "Mayor Henley, I'd like you to meet Kathy Sweeney."
  "Reverend Ellison, may I present Mr. and Mrs. Taylor."
  "Mr. Smith, this is Ronald Xavier, our temp worker for this week."
- Introduce a younger person to an older person:
  "Mother, I'd like you to meet Carol, my new roommate."

- Introduce men to women:
  "Susie, this is Richard Wright."
- Introduce guests to a host or hostess:
  "Jane, I'd like you to meet my cousin, Amy. Jane was kind enough to give this party."

Finally, don't worry if you turn around the order of an introduction. It's better to make an introduction of any kind than not to make one at all.

Q I have an awful time remembering people's names. Sometimes I don't remember the name of someone I've just met, and I'm too embarrassed to introduce them to anyone. What should I do in such situations?

A Ask the person to repeat the name if you don't get it when you first meet them. Then say the name back to be sure you have it right. Try to make some kind of mental association with the name. For example, if someone named Fred is wearing red, remember the rhyme. If a woman named Bean is skinny, use that association. Try to use the name several times in conversation. Finally, if you know you will see the person again or possibly pursue the relationship, jot down the name when you get home.

Q When someone I've just met mispronounces my name, may I correct them?

A Yes, but try to do so as pleasantly as possible. You might say, "My name is Bill, not Phil. They do sound alike, though, don't they?" If you have an unusual or difficult name and someone is having trouble with it, spell it for them or give them some mental clue that will help them pronounce it correctly.

Q I was recently upset when I began to make an introduction and couldn't remember the name of someone I had just met. This has happened to me before. At my daughter's wedding, I blanked out several times on the names of old friends. What can save the day when something this horrible happens?

A   First of all, relax. This situation isn't that horrible—or that rare. I suspect that you forget names under stress and then become even more stressed—which is no help at all—when you realized you have forgotten them.

First, try to get help from the person whose name you do not know. Do a kind of one-sided introduction ("Oh, hello, I'd like you to meet Mary Jones"), and hope that the person whose name you do not know chimes in with his or her name before you have to admit your error. When you're on the receiving end of this kind of half-done introduction, remember that it's a courtesy, if you get even a hint that someone doesn't remember your name, to give it before the other person stumbles.

If you've just met someone, it's only mildly embarrassing not to remember his or her name. Simply say, "I'm sorry, but I seem to have forgotten your name," which is the other person's cue to jump in with his or her name. You might sweeten your admission by adding something like, "I do remember that you are a Michigan State student, but I'm afraid your name has slipped my mind." If you are at a big party, you can always offer this excuse: "I'm afraid I'm just terrible with names when I meet so many people at once, and while I remember our conversation very well, I'm afraid your name eludes me."

If you can't produce an old friend's name, you obviously haven't forgotten it so much as you have blanked it out momentarily. Make a light joke of it: "Oh, I can't believe this has happened. Here I am, about to introduce my dearest friend, and my mind has gone blank."

· Male-Female Relations ·

Q   I'm a single woman, and I recently met a man I'd like to be friends with. That's all, just friends. What can I do about this?

A Call him up and invite him to lunch or dinner. Even if you were interested in something more, it's acceptable for a woman to take the lead these days—provided she is comfortable doing so.

Q In these days of equality, does the old "ladies first" rule still apply?

A It depends upon the kind of gathering and the ages of those gathered. Older men tend to offer women the small, traditional courtesies more than do younger men. Such courtesies are not often extended in a business setting when women are colleagues with men.

When men and women are together socially, most men still let women go through doors first, offer their arms if necessary to guide the women or help them down steps, help them on and off with their coats, hold their chairs for them, or open car doors.

In professional settings, a man is better off dispensing with most of these small courtesies, with the possible exceptions of letting women go first through doors and exit elevators first. Even these rules, however, should apply only when it is convenient. By this I mean that men should not step aside in a crowded elevator to let a woman elbow her way to the front and exit first. This is hardly a courtesy!

And in these days of egalitarian treatment between the sexes, I would remind women that they should open doors for men on occasion, particularly when a man is burdened with packages. Everyone, of course, should offer whatever courtesies they can to any elderly person, regardless of his or her sex.

Q I work hard all day long as a carpenter and then take a bus home. The bus is usually full of women who've been shopping all day. Am I really supposed to give up my seat for one of these women? I even resent giving up my seat for women who work.

If they want to work, let them stand just like I do most of the way home. That's real equality in my book.

A   In these days, when both women and men work very hard, men need not automatically give a seat on public transportation to a woman, but anyone—a man, a woman, and especially a child—should offer a seat to someone elderly or infirm, a pregnant woman, or a woman carrying a small child.

Q   How do I introduce the woman I live with?

A   There is no reason for you to point out the relationship when you introduce her to someone. Simply say, "Rona, I'd like you to meet Joan." If your relationship comes up in conversation, you need not hide it and might say, "Joan and I go together." You may even say that you live together, although most people exercise some discretion about to whom they say this. If you know your boss or your great-aunt Julie disapproves, sometimes it's better not to make a specific announcement.

Q   How do I introduce a date to someone we bump into while we're out together?

A   Avoid introducing anyone as "my friend Becky," since it's assumed that you are friends if you are together. You are under no obligation to explain your relationship when you introduce someone. Simple introduce a date this way: "I'd like you to meet Becky Riley."

Q   How much public affection is acceptable?

A   Virtually none. Friends may be greeted with a kiss and/or a hug in public, and a couple may hold hands.

2

. . . .

COMMUNITY LIFE

· Getting Acquainted ·

Q After years of living in the suburbs, I'm moving into the city, where I will be living in an apartment building. Are the rules for being neighborly going to be different?

A Despite a reputation for standoffishness, city people are just as friendly as anyone else, but since they live in such close quarters, they do play by different rules. For instance, you will probably find your city neighbors a little slower to make your acquaintance than your suburban friends. Don't mistake this, however, for permanent unfriendliness.

There are some things you can do to let people know you are open and friendly. Say hello to people when you see them in public spaces. Once they've learned to recognize you, they'll warm up. Be especially nice to two or three persons whom you spot as potential friends, perhaps offering a comment or two about the weather or your comings and goings. Eventually, you will make friends, and they will be just as close as your suburban friends.

Q We just moved into a new house in a new neighborhood. To welcome us, a neighbor brought over a pie she had baked. I need to return the pie dish, but I'm wondering if I'm obligated to put something in it. Or am I supposed to ask this neighborly family to dinner?

A The return of the pie dish does give you an excuse to call on your neighbor. It would be nice if you baked her a pie, but this isn't necessary. Nor need you invite your new neighbor to dinner. I would return the pie dish—and take along some store-bought cookies or sweet rolls if you don't bake—and talk for a little while. Your next step might be to invite the woman and her husband for drinks or dessert. And after that, if a friendship is in the offing, you will probably exchange dinner invitations.

· Children ·

Q My neighbor's children constantly run through my garden, trampling my plants. Their parents seem oblivious. What can I do?

A I would start with the children. Call them over to talk to you, and give them a little tour of your garden. Point out how the plants must be cared for, how some are very young and must be left alone. In other words, enlist their cooperation and interest in preserving your garden. I suspect they are running rampant because they don't know any better.

If this fails and they still trample your garden, talk with their parents about the problem. As is always the case when you complain to a neighbor, be as tactful and cordial as possible. Start by telling the parents how much you enjoy their children. You might even say that you suspect the children are unaware of what they are doing. Then ask the parents for their help in controlling their little ones. Don't make demands if you can ·possibly avoid it.

Q   I saw a small child heading toward a busy street the other day. His mother was calling to him but was too far away to stop him. I wanted to help but felt self-conscious touching someone else's child. People are so worried about their children having contact with strangers these days. What should I have done?
A   I know what you mean, but I think it would have been a kindness—if not a matter of safety—to have stopped the child. I can't imagine that a mother would be anything but apprecia-tive of such help.

Q   We live in a city apartment, with an elderly lady in the apartment below us. She has complained several times about our children, specifically when they bounce a basketball in the dining room and when the stereo is played loudly—or what she considers to be loudly. I'm at a loss over what to do. I can't keep my children quiet all the time just because we live in an apart-ment.
A   That's true, but you must realize that living in such close proximity to others creates the need for a few extra rules and regulations.
    Talk with your neighbor about her specific needs vis-à-vis your children. Does she sleep late? Go to bed early? Have trouble hearing the news on television during dinner hour because of the children's ruckus? Then negotiate a deal. Explain that you can't keep them quiet all the time and that, in fact, they do need to blow off steam at some point during the day, but that you will try to keep them quiet during the hours that are most important to her. As for your children, explain that there are times when they can be rowdy and times when they must be quiet. I think

it would be good to let them know that this is partly out of respect for others.

Q A friend of mine always assumes her children are invited whenever I ask her to dinner. Is she right?
A She's not. No one should ever assume that his or her children are included in a social invitation, and if there is any doubt, they should ask. It is the prerogative of the hostess or host to have an adults-only gathering. If your friends don't get the message, make it a little clearer. When you invite them over the next time, say, "Why don't you and Henry get a baby-sitter and come have dinner with us next Friday?"

If someone asks you whether an invitation includes children, and you have not intended it to do so, simply say, "Oh, no, they aren't invited this time. I thought we'd just have the grown-ups."

· Staff and Service People ·

Q I often get deliveries from the grocery store and drugstore. How much do these people expect to be tipped? More important, should I ask them to step inside while I get money for a tip?
A In a small town, where you know the delivery person, it is acceptable to ask him or her to step inside or even to carry your groceries to a kitchen counter. Tips are usually not expected, but it is kind to give one every so often. One or two dollars every few weeks will suffice, or you may give ten or fifteen dollars at holiday time.

In cities, a tip of fifty cents to one dollar is expected for each delivery. Delivery persons should not be invited inside, as a matter of personal safety. If you have tipped a delivery person year-round, it is not necessary to tip him or her something extra at the holidays, although some people like to give a dollar or two extra in the spirit of the holiday.

Q I just moved into a large apartment building, and I'm wondering what to tip the staff.
A Building employees do expect to be tipped. In fact, a list of employee's names will probably be circulated in November or December to help you plan your tips. There are two approaches to this. One is to tip the staff every time they do anything extra for you throughout the year. Another is to tip them well at holiday time and not tip them every time they do something extra during the year.

The amounts tipped vary widely from city to city and even from building to building, and you will need to check with some neighbors about what is an acceptable tip. To be polite, ask what amount they think is appropriate rather than what they tip.

Put the tip in an envelope with a personally signed greeting card. In some buildings, especially large ones with many employees, the tip money is given—in cash—to the building manager or supervisor, who will divide it among the staff. In some large buildings people do not tip the entire staff but only those from whom they have received services during the year. For more specific guidelines, see chapter 11, "Tipping."

Q I live on a pension and cannot afford to tip my building staff very much. I feel bad about this, especially since they are very good to me, always rushing to open the door and carry my packages. Have you any suggestions?
A No one should give beyond his or her means. Tip whatever you can afford—even one or two dollars per person. You might also consider giving small, handmade gifts, even baked goods, in addition to or in lieu of tips. I don't recommend this for

everyone, but I suspect the staff is aware of your circumstances and will appreciate any effort you make in their behalf.

·Ongoing Relations·

Q My husband and I are about to start some major renovation in our building. I am worried about noise complaints, particularly from a retired man who lives upstairs and is home all day. Any suggestions?

A Contact him before the work begins, and explain what you will be doing and how long it will last. Say that you hope he will not be too inconvenienced. A basket of fruit or bouquet of flowers delivered to him midway through and at the end of the project may also help to preserve your neighborly relations.

Q My neighbor has formed the habit of getting my mail from my mailbox and bringing it to me. She is more likely to do this when I have company or something is going on at my house that she wants to check out. I think she's just nosy. What do you think?

A I would agree with you, and besides, it's illegal for anyone to remove mail that isn't theirs from a mailbox. Still, it would be best to discourage her tactfully. Tell her you appreciate her getting your mail but that you really enjoy doing it yourself and would prefer that she leave your mail in your mailbox. She ought to get the hint, but if she doesn't, your next step might be to slip a note into *her* mailbox asking her please not to get your mail and reminding her that it is illegal to do so.

Q My neighbor drops in on me without warning. Am I obligated to ask her in and entertain her?

A You are not. In fact, one trait of a good neighbor is that he or she does not drop in uninvited unless you both have an understanding that this is an acceptable element of your friendship. Furthermore, even if you are at home doing nothing, you still need not feel obligated to invite in an unexpected guest. Say, "Oh, you've really caught me at a bad time. Let me call you tomorrow and we can arrange a time for a visit."

Q   We neighbor back and forth with some people who live kitty-corner from us. Are we obligated to ask them to every party we have?
A   No, you are not. If you entertain your family, for example, or a set of friends whom they do not know, it would be inappropriate to invite them. There are parties where it would be nice to include them: when you have other neighbors over, or when you entertain at an open house or some other large party.

Q   A woman stepped in front of me in the grocery-store line the other day. She pretended she didn't see me. I said nothing but seethed about it later. What could I have done?
A   For a start, don't seethe. It's far better to speak up—politely, if possible. When this happens to me, I say, "Pardon me, but I think I was in front of you in this line."

Q   I recently met a disabled person who couldn't shake hands with me. How should I have handled this situation?
A   When you see that someone won't be able to shake hands, you obviously don't extend yours. The same guideline applies to anything else a disabled person can't do: You don't do it.
Most handicapped persons today, however, do not like to be singled out for special treatment from others. They also don't like their disability to be ignored. While it would be rude to ask someone how he or she became disabled, it is equally rude to pretend someone's disability doesn't exist. Show an interest in discussing it if the other person initiates the discussion.

Q I frequently see a blind person at a busy intersection in my neighborhood. Often she is standing there, waiting for someone to help her cross the street. How do I do this?

A Ask her if she would like to cross the street with you. If she accepts your offer, let her take your arm rather than the other way around. Give her some warning when you are near the curb, if there is one, or the other side of the street. As you approach the other side, say, "Well, here we are."

Keep in mind, too, that blind persons are not the only persons who may need help crossing streets. The elderly often welcome the same attention, particularly when streets are icy.

Q I have a new friend who is deaf, but he reads lips. I'm not sure what is expected of me.

A Speak in a normal voice around your friend. Face him so he can see your mouth, and speak clearly.

As with any disabled person, let your friend set his own limits regarding where he will go and what he will do.

3

....

YOUR BUSINESS LIFE

· Getting Along with the Boss ·

Q My boss takes me out to lunch regularly (we discuss work), but I don't know whether I'm allowed (or supposed) to reciprocate.

A Generally, an employee does not invite a boss to lunch. The only exception is when you are very good friends—enough so that you know he or she welcomes an invitation from you. The fact that your boss discusses business when he or she takes you to lunch seems to indicate that you have more of a business than a personal relationship.

An employee is never obliged to reciprocate a boss's invitation either for a business lunch or a more social dinner in his or her home. Many bosses entertain their entire staffs at holiday time or on some other special occasion, and while they may even entertain them in their homes, this is still a business function and does not require that you entertain your boss in return.

If you are on particularly cordial terms with your boss and have been entertained in his or her home, however, you might ask him or her to an open house or some other large party that you are having.

Q   I have just started a new job, and I'm not sure whether or not to call people—especially my boss—by their first names. Can you give me any guidelines?
A   Be a little conservative about calling people by their first names. I would call your boss "Mr." or "Miss" (or "Mrs.") Jones until told to do otherwise. And it's not a bad idea to call any older people by their titles and last names, too.

Once you've been around for a few weeks or months, if you see that everyone but you calls these people by their first names, then you can probably safely switch.

Q   My boss has just invited me to a Labor Day picnic at his house. It's an all-day affair, and I would love to bring a date. May I ask to do so?
A   When an invitation is addressed to only one person (it does not, for example, say *Joan Lyman and guest,*), only that person is invited. When two people are married, living together, or otherwise involved in a long-standing relationship, both persons should be invited everywhere as a couple. Your boss, however, may not know that you have someone special with whom you share your life. If this is the case, say to him or her, "I'm involved with John Jones. Would you mind if I brought him to the picnic, or would you prefer that I come alone?"

I wouldn't push to include someone who is a casual date at a party in someone's home. If an office party is being given in a public place (where accommodations are not limited), and you know that other people are bringing partners, then I think you might simply say, "Do you mind if I bring a date, or would you prefer that I not?"

·Getting Along with Your Co-Workers·

Q I'm getting married soon. I can invite only seventy-five people to my wedding. While I want to invite a few close friends
from work, I don't want to invite everyone. Must I post a general
invitation inviting everyone? This seems to be the custom in my
office.
A You need not post an invitation inviting everyone. Some
offices do follow this custom, but you should do so only if you
can accommodate everyone who might decide to attend. Don't
forget, though, that you are inviting people to attend the wedding only, not the reception. In any event, most people will not
attend a wedding unless they are invited personally. Even so, to
be on the safe side, I suggest that you do not post an invitation
if your guest list is limited.
    Send invitations to your close office friends. Tell them that
you won't be able to invite everyone, and ask for their discretion
in not discussing the wedding at work.

Q I'm friendly with a woman at work, and we often do things
together after work. Recently, another woman has shown signs
of jealousy at not being included. How can we handle this?
A Office friendships should be discreet. If you see someone
outside work, or attend a party that some persons were not
invited to, it's kind not to discuss it in front of other persons—
who might indeed feel left out.

Q I've been working at a new job for several months now. How
can I thank those colleagues who've been especially kind to me
and who have helped me learn the job?
A I'm glad you want to thank them. It's easy to take the people
we associate with every day for granted. Why don't you ask each
person to lunch as your guest? It will give you an opportunity
to get to know them better and to show your appreciation.

You will be the host or hostess, of course, and you will pay for the lunch.

Q I have recently been promoted to a new position, and for the first time, I'm responsible for others' work. I know I'll have to be tough at times, but I'm also concerned about being nice. How can I let my workers know when I'm pleased with their work?

A Once you've exhausted the usual route of promotion and salary increase, I suggest that you write (or type) personal thank-you notes to people who have done something particularly well. I think you will find that you get a lot of mileage out of this very small gesture.

Q I'm having some co-workers to dinner at my house. My problem is this: I'm gay and live with another woman. How can I handle this? Should we pretend we don't live together? Or should I introduce her as my lover?

A Why not take a more middle-of-the road approach? You needn't pretend anything, nor need you hang a banner over the front door announcing your sexual preferences. Just introduce your companion by name. Some people will figure out the relationship, and some won't.

Q In every office where I've ever worked, some workers are loved and some are hated. What does it take to be popular with one's co-workers?

A It's easy to be popular with your fellow workers. The main thing to remember is to be a team player—always willing to help others and share what you know. Here is a list of traits that endear others to their colleagues:

- Treat everyone well—and equally. Be as nice to the night maid as you are to your boss and co-workers.
- Do your work. If you have the greatest personality in the

world, it won't help as much as will carrying your own weight. If you don't do your work, someone else may have to, or even if this isn't the case, those who work harder than you do will soon begin to resent your "coasting" or goofing off.

- Be modest. Don't announce every special project, every kudo you get the from the boss, every accomplishment.
- Don't apple-polish. Even if the boss loves you, it doesn't have to show—or better yet, it doesn't have to change your behavior toward him or others.
- Be punctual. People who show up on time resent people who don't. If you have some special arrangement that permits you to arrive late (and probably work late), make sure your co-workers know what's going on, and take care to plan your work so they are not inconvenienced by your late arrival.
- Meet deadlines. If a project is due on a certain date, make sure it is turned in on that date. If you cannot turn it in, let everyone who might be affected by the delay know.
- Be generous. Praise people when they deserve it, and offer lots of support when they haven't done so well. Share information that might be helpful to co-workers.
- Show interest. You don't have to be nosy to know when someone is having a birthday, has a child graduating from college, or has other cause for celebration. Stop by the person's desk even if you don't know him or her well, and offer your best wishes. If you know a co-worker has a special interest, ask about it from time to time when you find yourselves walking down a corridor or sharing an elevator or lunch table together.
- Stop short of nosiness. Few people like the office gossip or the person who is excessively nosy. Be sure it isn't you.

Q I'm just starting a new job, and naturally I want to make a good impression. Any hints on how I can do this?

A Yes, there are some guidelines that can help you get off to a good start on a new job. First, remember that you will want to have congenial relations with everyone, so be equally nice to everyone. While you're being friendly to everyone, resist joining any cliques until you have a sense of the office and its politics. You have at least a few months when you can feign innocence of any special groups or "power" alliances. Take advantage of this early period and use it to learn more about everyone before you form any impressions. More specifically:

- Greet everyone you see.
- Introduce yourself.
- Wait for people to ask you to join them for lunch. Some offices are friendlier than others, but all have their unwritten rules and social customs. On some jobs, you will be invited to lunch on the first day; on others, your co-workers will wait a while. Either way, try to let them take the first step.
- Be gracious to people who help you. Some of us have trouble in the role of beginner, but this is what you are on a new job, at least to some extent, so let people help you, and then thank them for their assistance.

Q A colleague who happens to be a good friend of mine was recently fired. I feel very bad about this, but I'm not sure what, if anything, I can do. Any suggestions?

A Offer your support. Spend extra time with your friend. Give him or her a pep talk as well as offering any leads or contacts you have that might help him or her find a new job. If you've ever been in a similar situation, you may want to compare notes. It's helpful for someone who has lost a job to be reminded that the same thing has happened to other people. This is one of the few times when people welcome advice from others and may even need it to bolster their egos so they can search for another job.

Q I'm about to get involved with a colleague at work. I know I shouldn't, but considering that I'm going to anyway, can you offer any advice on how to handle this situation?

A You're right, the best advice is, *don't*, but I have to admit that office romances aren't the rarity they once were and, these days, they often end with a lasting relationship and sometimes even marriage.

The best advice I can give you is to be discreet. Nothing provides better fodder for the office grapevine than a red-hot romance, and I suggest you give everyone as little to talk about as possible. How do you keep people from finding out about the office romance? Don't exchange loving looks. Don't touch. Don't spend any extra time together. Make your after-work plans out of earshot of others. Certainly, when the romance is in its early (and shaky) stages, never be seen arriving at work together, even if you spent the previous night with one another.

If the relationship becomes serious and steady, obviously you won't want or be able to hide it forever. If you're living together, you may come to work together in the morning, but even this can still be done discreetly. For example, don't discuss what you're having for dinner or which of you will pick up the dry cleaning while you're within earshot of others.

And if your relationship does turn into something perma-nent, you'll need to find out whether your company has any rules about nepotism. Some companies won't employ a married couple; others will. But even before you reach this stage, you may find it uncomfortable to work together. If this is the case, one of you can look for another job.

Q I'm a female executive with a lot of power, but one of the men who works for me continues to make a big show of gal-lantry—opening doors for me, putting his hand on my back to guide me, and making me enter and exit first from elevators. What's okay and what isn't? How can I tell him I would prefer to skip these amenities?

A How old is the man? Some older men are more comfortable showing women these small courtesies. Other men, of course, will do it to assert themselves in the face of your power. Finally, keep in mind that you may be getting these courtesy "perks" because you are the boss. Men tend to perform these same courtesies—minus the body contact—for their male superiors.

If you want to discourage it, however, start refusing to accept the little amenities. Hold the door for the man or, when he holds one for you, say, "No, you go ahead." If he doesn't get the subtle message, say something more direct, such as, "You know, Jack, while I appreciate your small attentions, I sometimes find them awkward at work. I don't mind your holding a door for me, but I don't think it's necessary. And sometimes, you should let me hold the door for you."

Q A colleague who's also a good friend recently got promoted over me. It's been hard to take, and I'm afraid I haven't reacted very well. What's expected of me?
A Your disappointment is understandable but no excuse for shabby behavior. When a friend is promoted or wins an award you were coveting, always try to be the first person in line to congratulate him or her.

Q I was recently promoted, and my best friend, who was also in the running for the same job, was not. What's my best move here? I want to preserve the friendship, of course.
A Continue as if nothing has changed. Go out of your way to spend some extra time with your friend. Realize, however, that he may not want to talk about what happened or, for that matter, talk about your promotion or new work assignments.

Ironically, at the very time when you're flying the highest about the company, your friend may be the most down on it and may even decide to look for another job. Offer as much support as you can. Encourage your friend to speak to your superior to find out why he was not promoted, and if the answer still makes him want to leave the company, then offer to read his résumé, share contacts with him—anything that will help him achieve his goal.

Q I've just gotten a wonderful fur coat. Do you think I could wear it to work?
A Only if you're a dogsled driver in the Arctic or a real estate broker in a northern city working in the dead of winter.

· *The Business Lunch* ·

Q I have to do a lot of entertaining for business. I've noticed that some of my "macho" male clients aren't too cool about a woman paying for their meal. Any suggestions?
A This is an increasingly rare problem, but I do have a couple of suggestions to ease both you and your clients over this awkward moment.

I suspect that two things trigger a man's impulse to buy a woman lunch when the situation should clearly be reversed: first, the presence of money, and second, the fact that the bill lands in front of him.

In the former instance, use plastic to pay, and in the latter, make sure that the bill is presented to you. You can arrange for this when you arrive at the restaurant by discreetly asking the headwaiter to give you the bill, but even better, simply by making it clear throughout the meal that you are the hostess. Do this by saying such things as, "Would you tell my guest what your specials are today?" or "My guest will have a white wine, and I'll have a Bloody Mary." If all else fails, you be the one to ask the waiter for the bill, and he will almost certainly give it to you.

If, despite all your efforts, you still sense that a client is uncomfortable with a woman buying his lunch, simply remind him that it is not you who is paying, but the company.

Q Who ends a business lunch—the guest or the host?

A There's no hard-and-fast rule about this: Whoever has an appointment or something to do that afternoon can be the one to draw a business lunch to a close.

The act of putting your napkin, lightly folded (but not refolded or crumpled) to the left of your plate or in the center of the place setting, if the plate has been removed, is one way to signal the end of the meal. At a formal dinner, the hostess signals her guests in this way that the meal is ended, but at business dinners and on other informal occasions, there is no protocol about who replaces the napkin first.

Q When I invite someone to a business lunch, is it up to me to suggest the restaurant?

A Yes, it is. Your guest will not know what price range or type of restaurant to suggest, and since you will be paying, it is up to you to hold the lunch in a setting that is comfortable for you.

Most persons who entertain frequently at lunch for business purposes find it convenient to settle on two or three restaurants they can use regularly. Another advantage to this is that they become known to the maître d' and waiters and often receive impressively excellent service.

Q A man with whom I lunch regularly for business purposes always takes me to a restaurant that serves a limited selection of heavy German food. I like it but have been trying to lose weight for months, and our frequent lunches don't help. Can I say something to him?

A I don't see why you could not mention your discomfort with this restaurant if this is someone with whom you lunch regularly. If you are not well acquainted with your host, however, I would not risk mentioning a diet as a reason to change the location of a lunch. It's too personal, I feel, and what's more, most people have grown a little tired of hearing that 80 percent of their fellow citizens are dieting. Please understand that I support efforts to diet; I just think dieters should keep their efforts to themselves, for the most part.

And before you suggest changing the lunch site (since this person must like it or he wouldn't go there so often), why not look over the menu extracarefully to see if there isn't something you can eat?

Q   When two people arrive from separate places at a business lunch, how are they seated? May the guest sit first or should he wait in the bar or front room until his host arrives? And what about when the situation is reversed: Should the host already be seated when the guest arrives, or should he be waiting at the front of the restaurant for his guest? I've had several occasions where this has been very confusing, with people waiting for one another in two different places.

A   The rules on this are pretty informal. The host can always go to his table to await the arrival of his guest for a business lunch—or any other kind of lunch for that matter. It is usually more convenient for him—and the restaurant—to go to the table. He should remind the head waiter or hostess that he is waiting for another person so the person will be brought to his table immediately.

When you, as a guest, arrive at a business lunch, tell the head waiter that you are the guest of Mr. Smith. He will, of course, take you to the table immediately if Mr. Smith is already there, or he may ask you whether you prefer to wait or be seated. There is no problem with your taking a seat at Mr. Smith's table before he arrives.

Q   When I am the first to arrive and be seated at a business lunch, may I order a drink or eat a piece of bread?

A   You may always order something to drink if you want to, but you should wait for your host to arrive before breaking bread or eating anything at the table. The one exception is when your host has obviously been held up and is truly late (i.e., more than fifteen or twenty minutes) rather than just a few minutes tardy. Then most hosts are more comfortable if their guests go ahead and eat something. Don't order from the menu, however, until the host arrives.

Q I'm French and I enjoy a glass of wine with lunch. But I find that many Americans do not drink at lunch. What are the rules about this? May I go ahead and order my drink or must I bow to the customs of my hosts, who usually do not drink at lunch?
A A few years ago, drinking at a business lunch was rare enough so that I would have suggested that you take a cue from your host and not drink if he didn't. Things are looser now, and I see no reason why you cannot order a glass of wine or other drink, provided your host has encouraged you to do so. You may do so even if your host is not drinking.

The one time I would not order a drink at a business lunch is when you are a job applicant. Even if your host drinks, I would beg off.

Q Is it permissible to share food at a business lunch? My friends and I often share interesting foods we have ordered when we dine out together.
A Strictly speaking, a business lunch is not a social occasion, and food is not shared. There are exceptions, though, one being when you eat at an ethnic restaurant where the sharing of dishes is expected. Most people, for example, share several dishes when eating Chinese food, and I see no reason not to do this at a business lunch. Food is usually brought on serving platters rather than on individual plates.

The other time you may want to share food is when one of you has ordered an extraordinary dish and is willing to give a bite or two to the other person. When food is shared in this manner, the person who is being given the sample passes his or her bread plate, and the sample is placed on the plate and passed back across the table.

One should never ask to taste another's meal; it must be offered. It is also perfectly acceptable to refuse a sample if you aren't inclined to share food with someone.

· Getting Along with Clients ·

Q   I've just taken a new job that involves much more client contact than my old job. I have an expense account and am supposed to entertain clients. My problem is this: I'm not sure when and how to do this.

A   Business entertaining is simple to arrange. It is mostly done at lunch, although you can also entertain someone at breakfast or dinner. Arrangements are made by phone. Telephone the client at work, which signals that this is business. You may choose the restaurant, but it's advisable to select someplace mutually convenient. Some of the occasions on which you will entertain clients are:

- To propose a deal
- To celebrate a deal
- To thank someone for something
- To talk about business
- To introduce people to one another

Q   Help! I'm a woman working in a man's world. I sell plumbing supplies, and my customers often call me "honey" or "dear." Is there any polite way I can let them know I don't like this?

A   The next time someone calls you "honey," smile and say, "Please, you can call me Joan." I'm pretty sure you'll hear a quick retort, such as, "Oh, are you one of those libbers?" To which you should reply (with a big smile), "Something like that, honey, but can't we still be friends?"

In other words, you'll jokingly let your client know this bothers you, he'll jokingly test the limits of your tolerance, and, if you're patient, he'll get the message and/or give up.

Q When must spouses be present at a business social function?
A Almost never, if the meeting is to discuss business. If you are hoping to establish a friendship or simply want to be on more intimate terms with someone, you might invite your spouses to join you. If one spouse is invited, everyone's spouse should be invited.

Q I travel to other towns and cities in the course of work and must entertain clients in each place. I'm not sure how to find good—or appropriate—restaurants wherever I go. Any suggestions?
A Ask your clients to suggest places where they might like to eat. If necessary, give them some clue as to the kind of restaurant you're looking for. You might say, "I'd like to buy you a nice dinner. What's the best restaurant in town?" Or: "Let's have a working dinner to discuss the new product. Can you recommend a quiet restaurant that serves good food?"

Q I recently read in the paper that the parent of a client of mine had died. I wasn't sure what is acceptable in a business relationship. I didn't feel close enough to go to the funeral, but I wanted to do something for this woman. What is appropriate in such situations?
A If you know the client well, you may attend the funeral, provided it isn't private, or you could send flowers. A condolence note is also appreciated by anyone who has suffered a recent loss. By the way, a business condolence note is the only kind that may be typed.

Such a note might read:

Dear Louise,
I was so sorry to read about your mother's death.
Although I never knew her, I know what it is to lose
someone you love. Please know that I'm thinking about
you in your time of loss. If I can do anything to help,
let me know.

Sincerely,
Rose

Q I have been given some business cards, but I'm not exactly sure how to use them. Do I offer them or wait for people to ask? Is it polite to use them at social functions?
A Business cards are used in two ways. The first is when you meet someone whom you think would be a good contact. In such cases, cards are usually exchanged. The second is when you are calling on a client. You usually present him or her with your card when you introduce yourself or, if the prospective client isn't in or can't see you, you leave a card.

Business cards are not used socially. For example, you would not tuck one in with a personal gift for someone. But you might give your card to someone whom you met at a social gathering.

· *Business Correspondence* ·

Q I'm an executive secretary who has returned to work after being out of the work force for many years. I need to know what to call people in the greetings to letters. Things have become much more informal than they were years ago.
A Use the name you would use if you (or your boss) were talking with someone in conversation. Persons whom you don't

know should be addressed, at least initially, as *Mr.* (or *Miss, Mrs.,* or *Ms. Tomlinson*), although most people switch to the more informal first names after a few exchanges of letters. This is okay among equals; when corresponding with clients on behalf of your superior, however, always err on the side of formality and use both the client's and your boss's titles.

Q How do I address a business letter to someone whose name I do not know?
A When writing to someone whose name you do not know, write *Dear Sir,* or if you wish to be nonsexist, *Dear Sir or Ma'am.*

Q Has *Ms.* become acceptable as a title?
A Yes, except in very conservative circles. Publishers still tend to think of *ms.* as the abbreviation for "manuscript," but the world at large has taken to this generic female title, which can be used for either a married or unmarried woman, and makes no distinctions as to her status.

Q I'm a recently married woman who has retained her own name. I've noticed that my secretary now closes my letters with *Mrs. Nancy Smith,* even though Smith is my maiden name. And several people in the office have taken to introducing me as "Mrs. Smith." Is this correct?
A It's not correct for your secretary to use any title in the closing of a business letter. Your name—Nancy Smith—should be typed, without title, under the closing, leaving room, of course, for you to sign your name.

In colonial America, any woman of a certain age was called "Mrs. So-and-So" as a term of respect, but today, "Mrs." is used only to designate a married woman who uses her married name. Married women who choose to use their own names are called "Miss" or "Ms."

4

YOUR PUBLIC
PERFORMANCES

· Public Courtesies ·

Q My husband has no sense of time and would always be late for live performances if I did not herd him along so we could be on time. When we are late, I'm so embarrassed. What can I do about this?

A It *is* rude to be late for any live performance, rude not only to the performers, but also to those who have come to see and hear them.

Have you talked directly to your husband about your embarrassment? I find that many people who are casual about time do not realize how much their tardiness inconveniences others. Instead of approaching this strictly from the personal point of view, point out that he is interfering with everyone's ability to enjoy a performance. One good trick I know to forestall tardiness is to set one's watch ahead five minutes or so.

Q I was recently a member of a very enthusiastic audience. When several persons began a standing ovation, the people sitting behind them told them to sit down. What do you think of this?

A That's appalling. A standing ovation is the highest tribute an audience can pay to performers. You are never obliged to participate in one if you are less enthusiastic than those around you, but it is the height of rudeness to ask those who do to sit down.

Q Could you explain when it is polite to applaud live performers?

A You should applaud at the end of every act and at the end of a performance. People also often applaud when the curtain opens on the set (especially nice if the designer happens to be in the house that night) and when the stars make their first appearance. Applause often erupts spontaneously after a beautifully sung aria in an opera, a monologue or other extraordinary bit of acting in a play, or a spectacular piece of dancing at the ballet. Applause that greets a star's entrance or rewards something extraordinary occurring on stage should be kept short so as not to interfere with the flow of the work. Although you didn't ask me, I think the custom of applauding at the end of a movie is silly. Who's there to hear it?

Q Aren't people who have coughing fits supposed to leave a movie or play? I hate it when I sit next to someone who coughs.

A Yes, the cougher should leave the theater until he or she gets the coughing fit under control.

Q I have great difficulty listening when anything interrupts my concentration during a performance or even a movie. That includes talkers, eaters of individually wrapped candies, and fidgeters in general. My problem is this: How do I let them know this is rude behavior without disrupting everyone else in the audience?

A It *is* rude to fidget, eat individually wrapped candies, or talk during any performance or movie—and unfortunately, it is increasingly common these days. When this happens, politely ask the person to stop the annoying activity. The next step, if necessary, is to enlist the assistance of an usher. It doesn't matter if others in the audience hear you asking someone to behave—they're undoubtedly troubled by it, too.

· Eating Out ·

Q Some restaurants have a sign that says "Please wait to be seated" and others don't. What is the right procedure in each situation?

A If you are asked to wait, then do so. In the absence of a sign or any indication that a host or hostess is at work, you may seat yourself. When a group enters a restaurant, one person—the host or hostess, if there is one—usually speaks to the headwaiter, who will want to know the size of the group and whether you want a table in the smoking or nonsmoking section.

The headwaiter leads the way to the table, and the women guests precede the male guests after him.

Q Six of us from work go out to a nice restaurant once a month. Our problem is one woman who smokes. If it weren't for her, the rest of us would sit in the nonsmoking section and be much happier about it. What is the fair thing to do in this situation?

A I go with majority rule. Since most of you do not smoke, I suggest that you sit in the nonsmoking section and that your smoking friend either refrain during the lunch or remove herself to a smoking area to have a cigarette.

Q If I don't like the table a waiter offers me, can I say anything?
A Of course you can. Simply select another table you find

more suitable, and ask, "Waiter, do you think we might have that table by the window?" If the waiter can, he will move you there, and if he can't (i.e., if the table is reserved), then be gracious and say, "Oh, then we'll take this table" and sit where he originally asked you to sit. You can also opt to wait for a better table if one will be free soon.

Q We think that some friends who ask us out for dinner—their treat—put us in an awkward situation. They do not drink and make a big deal out of it. But they always tell us to go ahead and order a drink if we want one. Needless to say, we're too sheepish to go ahead and do so. What is your feeling about this?
A I don't think we should bully one another with our values. Since they are the hosts, it would be a different matter if they didn't offer you a drink, but since they do, and since you want one, I would go right ahead and order one.

Q What's the difference between *table d'hôte* and *à la carte* on a menu?
A *Table d'hôte* means there is a set price for the meal, regardless of how many courses are served. On an *à la carte* menu, every item is separately priced. A *prix fixe* menu is the same as *table d'hôte*.

Q I get annoyed with waiters who rattle off specials, describe them in great detail, and never mention the price. Is it rude to ask?
A Absolutely not. Always feel free to ask a waiter how much a special costs.

Q After many years of living in Europe, I have come to enjoy my salad last—that is, after the entree. Is it acceptable to order it this way in restaurants?
A More and more Americans are learning to use salads the way

the French do—as palate cleansers, served after the entree. If you want your salad served last, tell the waiter when you order. He may or may not remember. If he doesn't, I recommend that you accept the salad anyway and simply do not eat it until you have finished your entree.

Q   I'm never sure what to do with all the paper containers food comes in these days in a restaurant.
A   Put them in the ashtray if there are no smokers present. Otherwise, put them on your bread plate or tuck them under the rim of your dinner plate.

Q   How should bread be eaten when a loaf of hot, unsliced bread is put down on the table?
A   The person closest to it slices two or three pieces, takes one, and passes it on. When all the sliced pieces are taken, the next person slices one for him- or herself and passes the loaf on. This way, the bread gets passed while it is still warm.

Q   What is a polite way to get a waiter's attention?
A   You should never clap your hands or whistle to get a waiter's attention, nor should you call out "sir" or "miss." Call out "waiter" or "waitress" if the person is within earshot. Otherwise, catch his or her eye and give a hand signal that attention is needed. Or you can ask another waiter to get yours.

Q   A friend of mine takes out a calculator to figure out the bill when three of us have lunch together. I think this is embarrassing and that we should just ask for separate bills. What do you think?
A   You can ask for separate bills, but you may not get them because some restaurants have a policy against splitting the bill for any one party.
    There is nothing wrong with your friend using a calculator.

Waiters often add up bills inaccurately, and smart consumers often double-check them.

Q I have a friend who always touches up her makeup before we leave the table. Am I right in thinking that this is the height of bad taste?

A It is fine to reapply lipstick and take a quick peek in the mirror, but this is all the grooming anyone should do in public. No one should ever touch up his or her hair during a meal, for obvious reasons related to sanitation.

Q How can two people share food in a restaurant? Is this bad manners in a good restaurant?

A Manners are manners and should be applied across the board. There is nothing wrong with sharing one another's food. In some Chinese and Indian restaurants, it is assumed that patrons will do so.

If you want a bite of food on someone else's plate, pass your fork so he or she can cut off a piece and pass it back to you. Anything more than a bite should be put on your bread plate and passed to you.

Q I always feel cheap ordering one dessert and two forks, but I can't eat much more than a bite or two of rich foods. Is this okay?

A In these diet-conscious days, no waiter blinks when asked to bring two forks. I suggest, however, that you ask for two forks and two plates.

Q How do I complain when food is ill-prepared? For example, we eat in one restaurant that serves fish far too rare for my taste. So far, I haven't complained because I know it's the way the chef does it, but I'm getting ready to.

A Food is far too expensive nowadays for any diner not to get what he or she wants, within reason. Graciously and firmly tell the waiter what is wrong and ask him to take back the dish. If the kitchen can't satisfy your request, order something else.

Remember to be equally generous with your praise when something is well done.

Q   How do I ask people to dinner when I want to pay? I'm a single woman who would occasionally like to treat a married couple, but they always end up treating me.
A   Make it clear at the outset that this will be your treat by saying, "I'd like to take the two of you to dinner."

Q   Aren't doggy bags taboo in a really good restaurant?
A   They're less commonly seen in fancy restaurants, but they aren't always taboo. If the waiter doesn't offer (and surprisingly often he does), ask, "Would it be possible to take this home with me?"

Q   I heard one never had to tip at a lunch counter, yet a friend of mine insists that we should. Which of us is right?
A   You should tip 10 to 15 percent at a lunch counter. After all, the server still has to serve you.

Q   How much should one tip the wine steward, and when is a tip required for him?
A   If the wine steward helps you choose a wine and serves it himself, you should tip him 15 percent of the wine bill.

Q   There's always a place for the headwaiter's tip on the charge slip, but I'm not sure when and how much to tip him.
A   Tip the headwaiter only if he has performed some special task for you, such as serving the wine or cooking something at the table. Give him five dollars or 5 percent of the bill, whichever is more.

· Travel ·

Q I dread train and plane trips because I don't like making small talk with strangers. Am I obligated to talk to a seatmate when I travel?

A If you want to send the message that you're not interested in chatting, settle into your seat and then busy yourself with some activity—reading, knitting, or note taking.

Seatmates usually nod and say hello when they take their seats, and there may be a few moments of polite conversation when the meal is served, but that is the extent of one's obligation to a stranger. If your seatmate persists in trying to carry on a conversation, you may smile and say, "I really can't talk. I have to finish this book [*or:* report, sweater I'm knitting]."

Q I'm going to take a cross-country train trip this summer. Is there anything I need to know? I'm especially unsure of what is expected of me in the way of tipping.

A Greet your seatmates when you first sit down, and excuse yourself as you exit or enter your seat. Seatmates should politely ask one another about shared amenities, such as lowering or raising a window shade, but you may keep your light on to read even after the person sitting next to you has turned off his or hers.

On long trips with a dining car, dinner reservations are usually needed and are made shortly after the train gets under way. Apart from that, a meal in the dining car is the same as a meal in any restaurant. You may share your table with a stranger, with whom you may or may not share some small talk. If you are traveling alone, it is acceptable to read throughout dinner if this suits you, even if you are sharing the table with someone— provided the someone, of course, is a stranger.

Tip the waiter 15 percent of the cost of the meal; you need not tip the porter who seats you.

Tip your car porter $1.50 to $2.00 a day, $1.50 a day for a long trip. Do tip another $1.50 to $2.00 for any extra services. Tip every two or three days if the trip is long.

Q I'm about to take my first transatlantic plane trip. Is there any special etiquette for plane travel?
A When you board, settle in as quickly as you can so others can do the same. If you need help reaching an overhead compartment, it's acceptable to ask another passenger or a member of the crew to assist you.

Seatmates usually greet one another and share a few minutes of polite conversation before they settle in to whatever they have brought along to do—and usually, to sleep for a major portion of the trip.

Meals will be brought to you automatically, and there is no tipping. You may or may not have to pay for the meal or drinks, depending upon the individual airline's policy.

Treat those who wait on you with the utmost courtesy. It is also a courtesy to the person sitting behind you not to move your seat too far backward, thus making it impossible for him or her to move very freely or rest comfortably.

· Religious Services ·

Q I'm shocked at what some people wear to church these days. I guess I'm of the old school—I still wear "Sunday best" to church. What is considered appropriate nowadays?
A Acceptable dress for religious services varies greatly from community to community and church to church, but conservative dress is still preferred. For women, this means dresses, skirts, a matched pantsuit, or a blazer or jacket and pants. Men wear shirts and pants (not jeans), a jacket and tie, or a suit, if custom dictates.

No one should attend a religious service wearing anything low-cut, shorts, T-shirts, or jeans, the sole exception being an outdoor or campsite service, where casual dress is permitted.

Hats are worn (for religious rather than fashionable reasons) only by Orthodox Jewish women. A guest generally follows the local congregation's customs with regard to covering his or her head. A non-Orthodox woman attending an Orthodox service, for example, would be expected to cover her head. Conservative Jewish men also cover their heads with yarmulkes during services, and guests may be expected to wear these; if so, they will be provided at the front of the sanctuary.

Q Must I follow the practices of another religion when I am a guest at a service?

A You should participate to some degree. For example, stand when others stand, sing or recite when others sing or recite, and pray (or at least stand respectfully) when others pray. Jews and Protestants at a Roman Catholic service do not kneel or cross themselves. Non-Catholics also do not take communion in a Catholic church, although some Protestant churches invite guests to share communion with them, and anyone who feels comfortable doing so may.

Any guest should make a contribution when the offering plate is passed. This is a way of thanking the church for its hospitality to you.

· Common Courtesies ·

Q I dread using public bathrooms because they are so often dirty. Have you got any suggestions that would help everyone keep public rest rooms cleaner?

A If we want clean public facilities, we must all do our part to keep them that way. Always wipe the toilet seat when you have finished using it. If a stall or rest room is out of toilet paper, report this to someone in charge.

·Q   I don't especially enjoy it when a stranger strikes up a conversation with me in public. Am I being stuffy, or is one obligated to talk to strangers?

A   You are not obligated to talk with a stranger, but there are polite ways of putting distance between yourself and the other person. Limit your responses to a minimally polite "Yes" or "No," and the other person will soon take the hint and take his or her garrulous personality elsewhere.

I personally do not always rule out giving strangers a chance, especially if they sound intelligent. I know two elderly women who have a close friendship of twenty years' standing. They met in New York on what is called the opera line—that is, standing in line waiting to buy tickets to the Metropolitan Opera—and now attend performances together.

5

· ·

ENTERTAINING AND BEING ENTERTAINED

·Parties·

Q I am invited to an anniversary party for an aunt and uncle. The party is being given by their children, who are in their twenties. My children, who are teenagers, are not included on the invitation. Would it be rude to inquire whether they are invited? They've always been included before.

A Since children are not invited unless their names are on an invitation, it *is* rude to ask whether they are invited. This is a family party, however, and you sound as if you have reason to suspect that your children may have been overlooked accidentally. I think you might make some tactful inquiries along the lines of, "Have you decided to make this an adults-only party?" or, "Are you just having the older generation for your parents' party?" If the response is yes, say no more.

Q I recently accepted a party invitation and then found out that I may not be able to attend. What do I do?

A As soon as you know you cannot attend a party you have accepted, call the host or hostess and withdraw your acceptance. If you then find out that you *can* attend, you may call back and ask if you can still come—provided the party is a large one. Once you have declined an invitation to a sit-down dinner, you shouldn't ask at a later date to attend because presumably your hostess will have invited someone else to fill your seat.

Q I recently received an invitation that says the dress is semi-formal. What exactly does that mean?
A What it means depends upon where you live. Men in semi-formal dress may wear black tie, or they may wear dark business suits. Similarly, the women may be dressed in short cocktail dresses or something much less dressy.

More accurate designations are *black tie* and *white tie*. Black tie is the equivalent of semiformal, and white tie, for which women usually wear long evening dresses, is the equivalent of formal.

Black tie for a man consists of the following:

- Black or white lightweight wool jacket, lapels trimmed in satin or grosgrain faille
- Matching black pants, without cuffs, outside leg seam trimmed in matching satin or grosgrain faille
- Matching vest or cummerbund (never both)
- White, front-pleated shirt with classic fold collar or white (not button-down) dress shirt
- Silk or satin black bow tie
- Plain black oxfords or evening pumps
- Thin black silk or nylon socks
- Optional: homburg, gray suede gloves, white silk scarf

White tie for a man consists of the following:

- Black tailcoat with satin lapels
- Matching black pants, without cuffs, outside leg seam trimmed in satin or grosgrain faille
- White waistcoat
- White wing-collared shirt with French cuffs
- White satin or silk bow tie
- Plain black oxfords or evening pumps
- Thin black silk or nylon socks
- Optional: silk top hat, white silk scarf, white gloves

Q   How far in advance should I mail invitations to a party?
A   Invitations to formal events should be sent four to six weeks in advance. For less formal events, send them three to four weeks before the party. Informal invitations, especially ones that are issued by telephone, can be made at any time but are usually issued a week to two weeks before the party.

Q   Will I hurt someone's feelings with a last-minute invitation?
A   If you are good friends and frequently entertain a person in your home, an occasional last-minute invitation is fine. The invitation that is always last-minute could be read as an insult.

Q   If I refuse an invitation, must I pay back the person who invited me?
A   No, because you haven't accepted his or her hospitality. If you are in the early stages of building a friendship, though, it's a good idea to pay back even an invitation you can't accept just to show your interest.

· Being a Host ·

Q   What makes a good hostess or host?
A   It is more work to be a good host or hostess than to be a

guest. Guests, after all, have hosts looking out for them. The best hosts and hostesses seem to have a second sense about others' comfort:

- They are there to refill the empty glass or to tuck a pillow behind the back of a guest who sits on a hard chair.
- Their guest rooms are comfortable because they themselves have on occasion slept in them.
- They offer drinks and seconds of food because they know that their guests, if they are polite, won't ask for them.
- They include all their guests in conversations—and if they spot someone alone, move to include him or her. They rescue guests who seem to have been cornered by a bore, and they ease guests out of heated arguments.
- They put their guests at ease by minimizing any accidents and glossing over any tactless or awkward moments.
- They are solicitous of their guests' comfort, and to that end, will encourage men to remove their jackets on a hot day, ask a newly arrived guest if he or she would like to freshen up, open or close windows or otherwise regulate temperature, and so forth.

Q A friend recently entertained me at a lovely luncheon at her club. I don't belong to a club and can't imagine how I can pay her back for this afternoon. Any suggestions?
A You can return your friend's invitation with one of your own, but you need not entertain her in exactly the same way that she entertained you. Although the general rule is that you should return an invitation with a similar one, this means only lunch—which can be held in a more modest club or restaurant or even at your home.

Q I was recently a guest at a huge, elaborate wedding reception. What do I do to pay back my hosts?

A Nothing. Large functions—weddings, showers, dances, anniversaries—impose no obligation to reciprocate with a similar invitation. How could you?

Q How long should I wait for a late guest at a dinner party?
A Since you don't want to inconvenience (or starve) your other guests, you need not hold up dinner more than thirty minutes waiting for a late arrival. Conversely, any guest who will be more than thirty minutes late for a dinner party should notify his or her hostess.

Q I have a friend who is a heavy drinker. How do I handle this when this person is a guest in my home?
A Hostesses used to be more timorous about dealing with drunks than they are nowadays. Frankly, a drunk is a danger to himself—and to others, especially if he drives. It is your responsibility to see that he doesn't.

Once you see that someone is inebriated, refuse to serve him anything alcoholic. Take charge of getting him home (and, yes, you can arrange for him to leave early) either by taxi or with someone who is willing to drive him. It is acceptable to take away the car keys of someone who is drunk.

Q I can't stand dirty dishes and often take time to wash them even when I have company. My wife thinks this is rude and that it sends a message to our guests that we want them to leave. Which of us is right?
A I agree with your wife. Washing dishes while you have company is a little like whistling "Goodnight, Irene, Goodnight." It's okay to wash dishes you need to use if you're short on wineglasses or dessert forks or plates, for example, but an extensive cleanup might be viewed as inhospitable.

Q When I'm the hostess, how can I end a party?
A There are several ways. For starters, close the bar, after first

asking everyone if they would like one last round. Take away the food, keeping in mind that it is inhospitable to mount a major cleanup effort while you still have guests in your home. Another tactic is to stop the music. You may also yawn or stretch— discreetly.

A hostess (or host) with overnight guests may always go to bed before her guests since she's usually up before they are.

Q   Am I obligated to entertain—or even invite in—someone who drops by my home uninvited? We have a neighbor whose curiosity must get the better of her almost every time we have company. She invariably "pops in" to say hello.
A   You are under no obligation to entertain uninvited guests. You need not even invite your neighbor to join you but may explain that you have company and will have to talk with her another time. If you have dinner guests, you may, if you choose, ask her to join you for a while, but if you can't stretch dinner to include another person, then you must simply say so and not feel bad about it.

If you are leaving to go somewhere when someone drops by uninvited, explain that you must leave by a certain time. It's helpful to be specific about when you must leave. Say: "We're on our way out, but I can talk to you for five (or ten, or fifteen, or whatever you can spare) minutes."

· Being a Guest ·

Q   I recently moved from a small town in Indiana to Chicago. The first time I was invited to a party, I arrived on time. Imagine my shock at being the only one to do so. I could tell the hostess was astonished, and there I sat, the only guest, for one solid hour. What are the general rules across the country about this?
A   In some communities, people go to parties later than the

stated time on an invitation—and in cities, this can mean up to an hour after the stated time. For sit-down dinners, city people often arrive anywhere from fifteen to twenty minutes late, depending upon local custom. To add to the confusion though, in some communities, invited guests are expected to arrive on time. You need to find someone to fill you in on the specifics of the community where you live.

As a general guideline, given a choice between arriving early or late, it is kinder to give your hosts the benefit of a few extra minutes' preparation time.

Q How long should I stay at a dinner party?

A You don't want to appear to eat and run, so an hour to an hour and a half is about the right amount of time to linger after dinner is finished. Of course, if a scintillating conversation develops, you may stay longer. It's also helpful to take a cue from your hosts, who did a lot of work to prepare the party. When they show signs of fatigue, it's time to go.

At a large party, you can leave at any time, since the party won't break up with your departure. At a smaller party, try not to leave until the party is showing signs of wearing down, in order not to break it up prematurely.

Q What makes a good guest?

A The key to being a good guest is consideration. More specifically, a good guest does the following:

- Shows enthusiasm for activities and people he meets
- Is courteous toward everyone, including servants and small children
- Displays good table manners
- Is able to occupy himself alone when his hostess and host are otherwise occupied
- Is able to make introductions graciously

- Is able to carry on a conversation
- Is an attentive listener
- Is respectful of the host's house and belongings
- Doesn't snoop but does display an interest in his surroundings
- Is cooperative
- Is discreet regarding what he hears and sees

Q Whenever we go somewhere, my husband lingers over his good-byes, and I tend to do them hastily—maybe too hastily. Can you give me some guidelines on this?
A Generally speaking, good-byes should be said quickly, especially if a party is still underway, so that you don't take your host or hostess away from his or her other guests for any length of time. After a large party, where you have barely gotten your host or hostess's ear to say that you are leaving, you may want to call him or her the next day to say how much you enjoyed the party.

Q How do I thank a hostess for a lovely dinner party?
A Even if the dinner party wasn't lovely, a thank-you call within the next day or two is obligatory. You need not call for a large party, but sending a card or note of thanks is a gracious touch.

Q I always offer to help my hostess and sometimes even go out into the kitchen to show that my offer is genuine. Is this okay?
A It's okay but perhaps unnecessary—and possibly unwanted. Many hostesses, particularly those working in small spaces, know how they want to handle the leftovers or stack the dishes and really don't want any help. At a formal dinner, you should never jump up to help your hostess, unless asked to do so.

Q When am I expected to take a hostess gift?
A If you dine regularly with old friends, a gift is not necessary

every time you get together, but you should take something every third or fourth time you go to dinner.

It's especially nice to take a hostess gift when the hostess is your mother or another relative, whose entertaining you often take for granted. We tend to overlook those closest to us, but mothers who prepare Thanksgiving, Christmas, and Passover dinners have surely worked hard enough to earn a hostess present.

For all others, a hostess gift is expected in most parts of the country. If you would like to take something besides the traditional flowers or wine, consider a small food gift, such as a jar of mustard, a bottle of vinegar, a canister of tea or coffee, or a small package of beautiful paper napkins or coasters.

Q I recently took a fine bottle of white wine to someone's home where I had been invited for dinner. I went to considerable expense and trouble to have the wine chilled and was disappointed when it was not served at the dinner. Don't you think this was rude on my host's part?
A Sorry, but your host is under no obligation to serve anything you bring to his home for the simple reason that it may not fit in with the menu he or she has prepared.

Q I'm the guest of honor at an upcoming dinner party. Do I need to arrive before everyone else? And is it true that I must leave before any other guests?
A Not any more. It used to be that the guest of honor arrived early and left early, but this rule no longer holds, with one exception. If you're the president of the United States, protocol dictates that no one may leave a party until you have retired.

Q I recently went to a wedding and was dismayed to find myself seated at a table with someone I dislike intensely. I quietly switched my and my husband's cards with those of another couple in order to put us at another table. Was I wrong to do this?

A Absolutely. I trust you will never do it again.

· Table Manners ·

Q What are the correct rules of placement for flatware?
A They're probably not so complicated as you might think.

For one thing, never put more than three of any one kind of flatware (forks, knives, or spoons) in a place setting.

Forks generally go on the left side of the plate, and spoons and knives go on the right side. (There are exceptions, such as an oyster fork, which may be placed with the forks or the spoons, but this won't come up in the basic place settings that most of us use most of the time.)

Flatware is placed in order of use; that is, a soup spoon goes to the right of a coffee spoon, and a dinner fork goes to the right of a salad fork if the salad will be served first, and to the left if the salad will be served after the entree.

Now for some of the fine points of place settings:

- The knife blade faces the plate.
- The bottom ends of the flatware line up.
- Dessert forks and spoons may be brought in with dessert, placed above the plate (the fork tines face the knife side, and the spoon faces the opposite direction), or put on the appropriate sides of the plate.

Q How do I use a dessert fork and spoon when both come with the place setting?
A Both the dessert spoon and fork are used to eat pie (or cake) à la mode and stewed fruit. In the latter instance, hold the fruit with the fork and cut off and eat a piece with the spoon. For pie

à la mode, use a spoon for the ice cream and a fork for the pie, although you may use the spoon to eat both, if you wish.

Q I'm stocking up on wineglasses, and my husband, who's a budding oenophile, tells me that there are special glasses for various kinds of red and white wines. We have a small apartment, and I'm not sure we have room for so many different kinds of glasses. Is there such a thing as an all-purpose wineglass, and are they acceptable?

A Purists—and those with large houses or apartments—do use different-shaped glasses for different wines, but few people bother with this nowadays, mostly for the reason you mention and because entertaining has become much less formal in recent years.

When space is a problem, I suggest that you buy a standard, all-purpose wineglass, one with a rounded bowl. Or perhaps you can compromise with one all-purpose glass and one specialized glass, perhaps a lovely set of dessert wineglasses.

I find it helpful to buy extras because wineglasses are always getting broken.

Q I've been given a lovely set of crystal champagne glasses. They are the wide, flat variety, and I understand these are in bad taste. Is this true?

A They are not in bad taste, but champagne aficionados believe that champagne is best drunk only in tulip-shaped glasses, which, they feel, better preserve the effervescence of the bubbly. I think this is a bit picky and that you should use—and enjoy—the glasses you have.

Q When can candles be appropriately used in a table setting?

A Candles may always be part of your centerpiece, but they are lit only after dusk, never during the daytime. They should be lighted shortly before your guests come to the table and may be extinguished as your guests are leaving the table.

Q I love the "unmatched" look in table settings, since I collect antique dishes and silver plate. Is there any right or wrong way to use these in a place setting?

A I agree with you that unmatched dishes and silverware can create a lovely table. The only guideline I can offer is that all the similar items should match. For example, you may use one set of dishes for your dinner plates and another for your salad plates, but all the dinner plates should be from the same set, and all the salad plates from the same set—unless you are very skilled at doing this sort of thing, in which case the rules are there only to be broken.

Q How should food be passed?

A At informal dinners, the best that can be hoped for is that all the food will be passed in the same direction. Strictly speaking, food is served on the left and removed from the right, so it is passed from left to right around the table.

Q I always panic a little bit when I'm confronted with a lot of silverware. How do I know which piece to use?

A There is a very simple rule to help you through this situation. Use the outermost fork or spoon first and work your way in toward the plate. If you're still unsure or encounter an unusual food, watch your host or hostess to see what he or she uses.

By the way, if you do use the wrong piece of flatware, don't worry about your error—it is a very minor infraction. You may quietly put down the wrong piece and start over with the right one or simply continue eating with the wrong one. Either way, don't make a fuss or even bother to comment on your error.

Q Where should I put used flatware?

A Always on your plate, never on the table. When eating food from a bowl, put the spoon on the service plate. If the bowl is wide and shallow, you may leave the spoon in it.

Placing your flatware diagonally across the top of your plate or together on the right side of your plate is a signal to your waiter or hostess that you have finished eating.

Q Should husbands and wives be seated together at a dinner party?
A If the group is large enough, eight or more, for example, then spouses are usually separated on the grounds that they speak to each other all the time and will find it more interesting to talk with someone new.

Q I like place cards and would like to use them. How do I do this?
A Place cards can be used at a formal or informal dinner. Use first names among friends. Titles and last names are used only on official or formal occasions, such as a diplomatic dinner. The place cards go in the center or to the right above the plate. They may also go *on* the plate.

Q When and how do guests who are gathered around a table sit down?
A The host or hostess stands until everyone has reached his or her place. The guests then wait for the hostess to sit first; a host waits for the women to sit down and then seats himself at the same time as the men. If the men hold the chairs for the women, they obviously sit down last, but these days, especially in a young crowd, everyone more or less seats themselves simultaneously.

Q If I don't use place cards, may I tell my guests where to sit?
A You may—and they're expected to sit there, too.

Q How long should I serve drinks before dinner?
A Cocktails are usually served for about an hour. Prolonging the cocktail hour is a little dangerous, as your guests, who will

be getting hungry, may tend to drink too much and eat too many appetizers.

Q May I take an unfinished drink with me to the dining room?
A Only if your host or hostess suggests that you do so. It's becoming more common these days, when people are drinking wine, to take one's wineglass to the table. Mixed drinks are rarely taken to the table.

Q I'm on a diet, and I've been invited to someone's house for dinner. Should I mention this to my hostess?
A If she's interested, your hostess will ask about your special food needs. If she doesn't ask, say nothing. Take small helpings of everything on your plate and eat what you can. A sophisticated hostess will not comment on your abstention. If you do not eat something for religious reasons, you may decline to put it on your plate.

If your hostess does ask, quietly tell her why you cannot eat it. She will undoubtedly make a mental note of this for future reference.

Q I was dismayed recently when weekend guests showed up and announced a rather long list of foods they did not eat— many of which were on my planned menu for the weekend. I was able to switch some items at the last minute, but not everything. We aren't talking about allergies here, but simply people who won't eat eggs or red meat. What is expected of the hostess in such situations?
A Everyone has become overly attentive to diet, if you ask me, and it does pose problems for hostesses and hosts. I think your houseguests should have alerted you in advance if there were certain foods they would not eat—and I think you did the gracious thing to adjust the menu when you could. You were also right to leave things alone when you could not change them. I hope you didn't worry too much about this.

Q Do table manners ever change?

A Indeed, they do. Elbows, once a "no-no" throughout a dinner, may now be rested on the table between courses, provided their owner does not slouch on them. Place settings have become much simpler, with fewer plates, glasses, and pieces of flatware.

Sometimes, something old even reappears. This is happening now, with something called a *sauce spoon* that is showing up at individual place settings for some formal dinners. Because we're all so diet-conscious, few people use bread to soak up sauces any more, so the sauce spoon—a flat piece—is used instead.

6

. . . .

THE ART OF GIVING
AND RECEIVING

· Giving ·

Q   I just received an invitation to an anniversary party for some very dear friends. The invitation reads, "No gifts, please." Does this mean I can't give a gift to these people even though I was planning to anyway?

A   You can still give a gift. "No gifts, please" can be loosely interpreted to mean "please don't bring a gift to the party." Family and close friends who were planning to give the couple a gift anyway may still give one. They should drop by the couple's house a few days before the party with the gift.

Q   Are people supposed to open gifts at a party? I recently attended an anniversary party where everyone brought presents, but they were set aside and—I assume—opened later. Frankly, I was disappointed.

A   Sometimes gifts are opened at parties, and sometimes they are not. Gifts are not opened at very large parties because it would take too much time away from the fun of socializing and dancing. This means, in effect, that presents are not opened at weddings, large anniversary parties, bar mitzvahs, and similar parties.

They are also not opened at parties where some guests have brought presents and others have not. When only some of the guests bring gifts, they are set aside, to be opened later.

At other parties, such as baby and bridal showers, and birthday celebrations, the opening of the presents is a highlight of the party.

Q I never know what kind of present to give someone. I've been told that I should give a present I would like to receive, and I've also heard that I should ignore what I would like and give something that the other person likes, even if it isn't to my taste. Any suggestions?

A I personally lean toward finding presents that I think the other person would like and that I also find tasteful. (One exception: Like most mothers, I didn't understand my teenage daughter's taste as she was growing up, but I deferred to it and got her what she wanted rather than what I thought she should have.)

To find out what others would like, you need only listen to them talk about their lives. What are their hobbies? What do they read? What kind of music do they listen to?

Observing a friend's style of dress and the decoration of his or her home will also offer countless clues for the kinds of presents he or she would like to receive. Does your friend collect antiques? Buy something old, or something that looks old, as a present for him rather than something shiny and modern-looking. Does your friend accessorize her clothes with interesting scarves and jewelry? Look for gifts like this.

The reverse is also true. If you note that a friend never wears jewelry or reads a book, then neither of those things would be welcome gifts.

Q   Is money ever an acceptable present? I've been told it is, but I have my doubts and don't like to give it.

A   In some social circles, money is an acceptable and even welcome present for a wedding, a bar mitzvah, or a confirmation. It may be particularly welcome at a wedding anniversary for an elderly couple who are living on a limited income or who have reached a stage in their lives where they have little use for additional possessions.

If the idea of giving money rankles, consider a gift certificate instead or, especially for a youngster, a stock or bond.

Q   I've been told not only that I should give money (something I never do) at an upcoming anniversary party, but that the amount I give should be based on how many of us are attending the party. For example, my husband, myself, and our son will be going to the party, and it was suggested that we give fifty dollars a head. My cousin said that would cover the cost of feeding us. What do you think of this?

A   I think it's the most ungracious idea I've ever heard. I urge you to resist this kind of pressure and stick to your usual form of gift giving. Even if you were to give money—and you should do this only if you thought it was what the couple wanted—you should give whatever you would spend on a present, and that is often based on what you can afford or feel is appropriate.

Q   I recently left a present on the gift table at a niece's confirmation. I gave her a nice pearl ring, but now several months have passed, and I haven't heard anything from her. I'm worried that the gift was lost or stolen. Would it be rude for me to ask?

A   That is exactly what your concern should be if someone has not responded to a present after several months—and exactly how you should word your note inquiring about it.

Q   I am an elderly woman living on a pension, and I have a large circle of friends, many of whom are better off than I am. They would all like to exchange holiday gifts and so would

I—but I can't afford it. I can't even afford birthday gifts for everyone. Any suggestions to help me out of this bind?

A   Yes—explain your situation before the need to buy a present arises. Simply say, "I wish I could afford to buy all the gifts I would like, and I hope you'll understand that I can't exchange holiday (or birthday) gifts with you."

Alternately, you might try to find or make very small gifts. (It doesn't matter if your friends want to indulge you with more expensive gifts.) Or think about a token gift: a single flower or a book you've read and loved and want to pass along permanently to a friend. You could also give a gift of your time: Offer to help a friend grocery shop or to accompany her to the doctor or some other appointment. A gift of time is one of the most important gifts you can give.

Q   I've just started dating someone. When we go out, he always pays. I've been thinking that I would like to return the favor somehow, possibly by giving him a special present. I was thinking of buying him several ties. I know he hates to buy clothes and thought he might appreciate someone helping out. Would this be appropriate?

A   Your instinct to repay him with a present is on the mark, but I think you should skip the ties in favor of something a little less personal, especially if he hasn't given you any similar presents yet.

First, try offering to buy him dinner. Many men are quite gracious about accepting this kind of turnabout. If you want to do something else, stock his refrigerator with a nice food or beverage present—or both. Try a few unusual beers or a bottle of liquor, if that's his preference, or some fine wines and a hunk of cheese, nicely wrapped, along with a box of crackers. If he loves a certain kind of candy, buy him some. Gifts of clothes and housewares are too domestic for many men, especially at the start of a relationship, but a record or book he's been wanting may strike just the right note.

Q A man I date just got a big promotion. Would it be appropriate to send him flowers as a congratulatory gift?

A. Yes, I like the idea of a woman sending a man flowers. You might consider something "masculine"—birds-of-paradise, large chrysanthemums, or African daisies, for example.

Q I'm crazy about this woman I've been dating for only a month or so. Her birthday is coming up, and I'm thinking of splurging on a really good watch or some other piece of jewelry. Would this be appropriate?

A It's old-fashioned of me, I know, but I would hold off on an intimate or expensive gift until you have a more established relationship. Even when your intentions are the best, a woman may find it awkward to receive such a gift when she hasn't known you very long.

Q I don't think people send flowers much anymore, but I'd like to start. When are they appropriate?

A Flowers are a wonderful gift and are appropriate on many occasions: birthdays, anniversaries, before and after parties (to thank the hostess), to welcome, to congratulate, and always to thank someone for a special favor.

· Receiving ·

Q When I had an open house last Christmas, several people brought presents even though I don't ordinarily exchange Christmas gifts with them. I was embarrassed since I had nothing to give them. What should I have done?

A There are two possible ways to handle this situation. One is to have ready several small presents already wrapped and waiting for those persons who give you a gift unexpectedly. A small homemade present or a gift of food is ideal for such occasions.

The second option is to treat these gifts as hostess presents, which I suspect they mostly were, and not reciprocate.

If someone gives you a gift and you do not want to begin exchanging gifts with them, simply accept the present graciously and comment, "This is lovely, but you really needn't have gotten it." If you can't stand not to return the favor, buy your friend some small present and give it to him or her at some time during the year *other* than when a gift was given to you. You will have repaid the favor without setting up a ritual gift exchange—and you will have done so when your budget could most afford the extra cost.

Q   Is it okay to exchange a gift I don't like?
A   It depends. In general, duplicate gifts—especially wedding gifts—may be exchanged, since no one needs three or four toasters. Gifts that are the wrong size or the wrong fit may be exchanged. A book you've already read may be exchanged. Whenever someone gives you a present and tells you to exchange it if it isn't right for you, then you may take him or her at his word and assume there will be no hurt feelings if you exchange it for something else.

But if your Aunt Louise gives you a wall hanging that she thinks is art (and you think is dreck), I'm afraid you are stuck with it. For one thing, it's hard to cover up the fact that you've exchanged a one-of-a-kind gift, and it's hard to come up with a reason—other than not liking it—for doing so.

You must never appear anything less than gracious and delighted with a gift—no matter what you really think of it.

Q   I recently exchanged several duplicate wedding presents. How do I handle this with the persons who gave me the presents?
A   If possible, say nothing. If they notice or ask about their present, you may have no choice but to acknowledge that you

exchanged it. Reassure them that you did so because it was a duplicate, and tell them what you got—and how pleased you are with it—in exchange.

Q I received a beautiful crystal bowl as a wedding present, but it was chipped. Do I tell the donor and ask her to replace it?
A Not if you can avoid it. If you know what store the present came from, deal directly with them. If you cannot return it to the store, see if you can get it fixed, and if not, then you may have to dispose of it, perhaps by giving it to some charity. Only if pressed by the donor should you acknowledge that the gift was damaged.

Q Friends give us (we're a family of four) individual gifts at Christmas, and we give them a household gift. Frankly, we can't afford to give them separate gifts, but I always feel bad about it. Any suggestions?
A Don't waste another minute feeling bad. One should always give what one can afford. Your friends, whom I assume are wealthier than you are, obviously know that they could give you one household gift and still choose to present individual gifts. They do what they're comfortable with, and you should do what you're comfortable with. I'm sure they never give it another thought—and neither should you.

7

· ·

WRITTEN
COMMUNICATION

·General Correspondence ·

Q I am moving soon. How do I announce my new address to friends?

A You may announce your new address in one of three ways, the latter being the easiest and most frequently used method by those who don't have quite enough time to live in the style they would like:

- Through printed announcements
- Through personal notes
- On your Christmas cards

Printed announcements can be the preprinted variety or more formal ones printed especially for you. With the preprinted announcements, you simply fill in the blanks. More formal change-of-address cards are worded as follows:

> Mr. and Mrs. John Carter have moved.
> Their new address is
> 32 Rolling Hills Court
> Plainfield, Indiana 46820

Alternatively, and somewhat more formally, a printed announcement might read:

> After April 10
> Mr. and Mrs. John Carter
> will be living at
> 32 Rolling Hills Court
> Plainfield, Indiana 46820

Or:

> Mr. and Mrs. John Carter
> have changed their address to
> 32 Rolling Hills Court
> Plainfield, Indiana 46820

If you don't have a wide circle of friends and acquaintances to inform of your move, you might enjoy sending short notes on your informals (see the following question). And as I suggested, if you're as busy as the rest of us, and your move occurred any time after late summer, you can also spread the news via your Christmas cards.

Q   What are informals and how are they used?

A   Informals are folded-over notes, large enough to meet the post office's minimum mailing requirements of 3½-by-5 inches, printed or engraved with either your name or monogram.

They are used for any form of short correspondence, but especially for thank-you notes and invitations.

Q   A friend told me my informals are incorrect since they are printed with only my first name.

A   She's right. Informals printed with only a first name are appropriate only for young children.

Q   My husband and I use different names, yet we would like to have joint stationery. Any ideas on how we can do this?

A   You could have a "house" stationery printed with your address only, or you could, at extra expense to yourselves, have a joint monogram made up and used on engraved or printed stationary. I would combine your last names rather than both your monograms. Something like this could be very attractive:

$$\mathcal{F} \infty \mathcal{W}$$

Q.   I would like to give a recent college graduate some writing paper as a gift. What do you suggest?

A   An all-purpose paper is best. Writing paper ranges from 8½-by-11 inches down to smaller sizes. Consider having the paper printed or engraved with the recipient's name or monogram and address.

If you want to give your friend a complete paper "wardrobe," I suggest the formal writing paper I just described plus some informal or one of the new, interesting kinds of stationery such as preprinted postcards.

Most stationery stores stock an interesting and varied supply of writing papers that can be ordered. Don't forget, you will need six to eight weeks to order specially printed writing paper.

Q   Are preprinted address labels acceptable? I find them very convenient but also think they are probably very informal.
A   It is okay to use preprinted address labels. The post office prefers that the return address be placed on the front of an envelope, but this is not possible with engraved stationery and doesn't look particularly good on personal stationery.

Q   Do I need calling cards?
A   Probably not. Calling cards—formally printed white or ivory cards bearing your name—used to be de rigueur for most people but are no longer used except in the military, where formal calls are still made by persons above a certain rank. Their only other use is as gift enclosures, but most people today buy preprinted cards or use their informals.

By the way, if you use your informals as gift cards, you should write a message on the inside. If you do decide to order calling cards and use them as gift enclosures, no message is necessary, strictly speaking, but it is warmer to write a personal line or two—always on the front of the card.

Q   I give up on modern titles. My nephew just married a woman who is keeping her name. However do I address letters to them? Is she *Miss, Ms.,* or *Mrs.?* Can't I just dispense with all these titles. At seventy-eight, I'm willing to make this very modern move. What do you think?
A   You are not alone in thinking that titles have become too much of a bother, and some egalitarian souls do indeed dispense with titles, addressing their letters simply to *Jane Jones* or *Simon Smyth,* regardless of the person's marital or professional status. (It also seems odd to me to address lawyers of the female persuasion as *Esquire,* but it is perfectly correct.)

As for your more specific problems, your new niece-in-law is addressed not as Mrs., because she is not using her husband's name, but as Miss or Ms.—whichever you prefer.

Q Now that I am married, do I sign my name and my husband's name to correspondence—our thank-you notes, for example?
A For handwritten notes and letters, only the name of the person who actually wrote the note is signed, although you may write on behalf of both of you. For example:

> Dear Aunt Sally,
> John and I would like to thank you for the beautiful
> vase. We love the color and shape. You were wonderful
> to remember us so generously.
>
> > Love,
> > Beth

The exception to the one-signature rule is cards for special occasions and holiday cards. Either spouse may sign for both.

Q I am married but will continue to use my maiden name. How do I sign my personal correspondence? Am I Ms. or Mrs.?
A You are not Mrs. since you are not using your husband's name. You may be either Ms. or Miss, according to your preference.

Q How do I address letters to young children? Has Master fallen completely out of use?
A Until about age ten, little boys' correspondence may be addressed to Master William Wiley. Little girls' mail is addressed to Miss or Ms.

Q How do I sign personal letters? Must I always sign them Love? I notice that everyone signs everything this way now, and the closing I was taught—Affectionately or Fondly—seem stilted.

A *Love* has proliferated in our society, hasn't it? I, too, balk at the idea of signing a letter *Love* to someone who is less than a dear friend. I close letters to acquaintances with *Fondly* or *All the best.*

Q I am furious with a friend who is dating an ex-boyfriend of mine. I want to write her a letter and let her know just what she has done to destroy our friendship. Should I do it?
A I urge you not to write—or, if you must write one, not to mail—an angry letter. While a letter or note may be an acceptable way of communicating your displeasure with a friend if you cannot speak with him or her directly, an angry letter is something else. They have a way of popping up at inopportune moments in our lives and embarrassing us with their overwrought emotions.

Think twice before writing an angry or overly emotional letter to anyone.

Q I have arthritis and am elderly. Can I type my personal letters? I was brought up to think this was wrong, but it's the only way I can keep up with people.
A You absolutely may type your personal correspondence. It's quite acceptable these days except for condolence notes, and even then, I think you might type yours and explain briefly why you are doing so. Etiquette is supposed to make life easier for us all, and it would be a shame if you gave up staying in touch with people, which you obviously enjoy doing, over a small point of etiquette.

· *Invitations* ·

Q My husband and I have been invited to a wedding reception, and only I can attend. First, is it proper for me to go without my husband and, second, how do we respond in writing to this situation?

A One of a couple may always attend a large function without the other—and one also hopes that hostesses nowadays are liberated enough to encourage one person to attend small functions, even if this does leave an uneven number at the table.

As for answering the invitation, which is, I assume, formal, this is the proper wording:

> *Mrs. William Smyley*
> *accepts your kind invitation*
> *but regrets that*
> *Mr. William Smyley*
> *will be unable to attend . . .*

Q How do I respond to an engraved, formal wedding invitation? I've asked a few people and gotten all sorts of answers. I feel awkward writing a formal response, since the bride is my favorite niece and we're very close. I don't want to seem distant.

A There are three possible ways to respond to a formally worded invitation:

- Use an enclosed response card.
- Write a formal response.
- Write an informal response.

You may use a response card if one is enclosed. Until recently, I, like most other etiquette experts, found these in somewhat questionable taste, but not responding to invitations is in worse taste, and since it seems to have become the rule rather than the exception these days, formal response cards have become a necessity.

To use one, fill in whatever information is requested, slip the card into the preaddressed, prestamped envelope, and mail it back. I urge you to use the response card whenever one is enclosed. They make life easier for the bride.

If no response card is enclosed, then you should respond with a formal response note. It should be written on white stationery in blue or black ink, paralleling the wording on the invitation:

> *Mr. and Mrs. George Sawyer*
> *accept with pleasure*
> (or)
> *regret that they are unable to accept*
> *Mrs. Berkeley Jamison's kind invitation*
> *for Tuesday, the sixth of June*

You need not repeat the year or the place and time.

Finally, if you are unusually close to the person who sent you the invitation, as you suggested, you may feel more comfortable responding with an informal note—on your regular or informal stationery. For example:

> *Dear Merrilee,*
> *Since you are my dear niece, I could not think of sending a formal response to your wedding invitation. Don and I will, of course, be at your wedding— beaming with happiness.*
>
> *Much love,*
> *Aunt Bessie*

Two other possibilities are to send the formal response along with a kind, loving note.

Q   I just received an invitation to my sister's wedding, complete with a response card. I am going to be her maid of honor, so she knows I will be at the wedding. My question is this: Must I answer the invitation?

A Of course not. You were sent the invitation as a memento.

Q When is it acceptable to use preprinted invitations? I've heard they can never be used for a semiformal or formal occasion, but my sister and I are planning a large cocktail party for our parents fortieth wedding anniversary, and we've found some wonderful invitations we would like to use.

A I think preprinted invitations are wonderful. Many have beautiful, creative designs. I use them for all my dinner parties, but a young friend tells me that they would be considered affected in her circle, where the custom is to telephone all but the most formal invitations.

You may use a preprinted invitation for any occasion except a formal event such as a wedding or when time is too short and invitations must be telephoned. They would be perfectly appropriate for your parents' party.

Q Are reminder cards ever appropriate? More than a month ago, I invited eight friends to be my guests at a charity dinner and ball. Needless to say, I am paying for the table, and I would be upset if someone "forgot" to attend.

A Reminder cards are an excellent idea whenever you have invited people several weeks in advance or when the invitations were telephoned. Use your informal stationery or some other attractive writing paper. Simply write:

> *To remind you—*
> *Dinner, Wednesday, January 5, 8 P.M.*

Q May I use my informals for invitations?

A Yes, that's exactly what they're intended for, among other things. Write the invitation around your name:

```
┌─────────────────────────────────────┐
│          Cocktail buffet            │
│        Mrs. Wilbur Lawson, III      │
│          Sunday, October 3          │
│             5 o'clock               │
│          1250 First Avenue          │
└─────────────────────────────────────┘
```

Alternatively, you might write the invitation on the inside:

Dear May and Howard,
  Could the two of you join us for cocktails and buffet
supper on Sunday, October 3, at 5 o'clock at our
home, 1250 First Avenue? We look forward to hearing
from you and, even more, to seeing you.

                                        All best,
                                        Constance

Q What is the difference between an informal and fold-over notepaper? Can't they be used for the same thing? Should they bear my name and my husband's or just my name? Can I use a monogram? And finally, what are they used for?
A Your confusion is not surprising. True informals—small, folded note cards bearing your name or monogram—have largely been replaced by the larger fold-over notepaper, mostly because post-office regulations require that all mail be at least 3½-by-5 inches. You may have either your name or your monogram printed on an informal or on notepaper.

These days, they are used for the same things: short notes, thank-you notes, and informal invitations.

Q My husband and I are planning to entertain fifty of our friends and family at a dinner dance on our thirtieth anniversary. Would engraved formal invitations be appropriate?

A You may send engraved formal invitations if the occasion is a formal one—either black or white tie. If your party will not be so .formal, think about preprinted or printed informal invitations or invitations done especially for the occasion by a calligrapher.

Q How do I get people to respond to a big party I'm planning?
A Make sure the invitations include a response line that reads either *RSVP* or *Please respond.* You may, if you wish—and if it is necessary for your planning—designate a date by which you would like people to respond. Two addresses may be included on the invitations: one for the responses and one designating the place of the party.

Alternatively, you could enclose a response card along with a self-addressed, stamped envelope.

Q What kinds of invitations are appropriate for a six-year-old's birthday party?
A Almost anything that is informal, colorful, and cheerful. There are many charming, preprinted invitations that would be perfectly appropriate.

Q I am having a small, informal wedding and would like to hand-letter my own invitations. My mother says this is highly improper, but we have agreed to let you decide.
A In these days, when wedding invitations have taken a turn toward the informal, I see nothing wrong with a hand-lettered invitation to an informal wedding. I would caution you against anything overly sentimental or otherwise inappropriate, though. A wedding invitation, formal or informal, should be dignified, as befits so momentous and meaningful an occasion.

· *Thank-You Notes and Other Must-Write Correspondence* ·

Q When is a thank-you note necessary? Some people write them on occasions when I wouldn't dream of writing one, such as when I have just opened a gift in the presence of the giver.
A A thank-you note is required on the following occasions:

- When you are a guest of honor at a dinner (thank your host)
- When you are an overnight (or longer) houseguest
- When you receive a gift and haven't thanked the giver in person
- When you receive a shower present from someone who wasn't present at the shower
- When you receive a congratulatory note
- When you receive a hostess gift sent after your guests have departed
- When you receive a wedding gift

Q How do I thank someone for a gift of money? Should I mention the amount in my thank-you letter?
A You need not mention the amount, but you may if you wish. It is also kind to indicate how you might use the money. If you will buy something specific, say so; if not, indicate in some general way how you would use the money, perhaps by saying something like this:

> *Your generous check was most appreciated. Bill and I have put it into our special account earmarked for a new sofa.*

Q I am ten, and my mother says I must write my own thank-you notes this year. What do I say, especially if the present is a dumb one?

A Writing thank-you notes can be fun. Remember, they make the receiver feel very happy about sending you the present.

I do agree that it is difficult to write a thank-you note for a present you do not particularly like, but it must be done. See if you can't pick out something that's nice about the present. If you don't like the style of a sweater, for example, write about how much you love the color.

If you just don't like anything about the gift, I hope you'll still try to find something nice about it. On rare occasions, we tell small white lies like this in order to save another person from feeling unnecessarily bad about something.

By the way, your thank-you notes should be written and mailed within two or three days after you receive a present, unless the occasion was very big and you received many gifts. Then you may take up to three months.

Q I haven't received a thank-you note although I sent a friend a wedding present over four months ago. I'm worried that the gift didn't arrive or arrived without a card identifying me as the sender. Would it be rude of me to ask?

A After so long a time, you must inquire about your present because there is every possibility that something did go wrong. Write or call the bride or groom and explain that you sent a gift but are worried about it. You will either receive a very logical explanation or a very embarrassed note of apology over the delay.

By the way, if the gift did not arrive in good condition, the recipient should return it to the store where you purchased it. You may offer to help with this but are not obligated to do so.

Q When are preprinted cards acceptable?

A I continue to campaign for personally written notes in this age when so few of us indulge in any written correspondence, but I am aware that a lovely selection of preprinted cards exists, and I buy birthday, graduation, baby, First Communion, congratulatory, and many other preprinted cards. I do try to add a personal message to all preprinted cards.

Q When are letters of congratulation necessary? May I type a personal letter of congratulation?

A You are never obligated to write a letter of congratulation in the sense that you are to write a thank-you note. I find letters of congratulation a pure pleasure to write. They are sent for any of the following occasions:

- Engagement
- Wedding
- Birth of a baby
- Promotion
- Any special achievement

You may type or handwrite a letter of congratulation, although I think a handwritten note adds a special touch.

Q My husband's family, all of whom live in the same town we do, send cards for every conceivable occasion, including holidays that we get together to celebrate. I can't keep up—I can barely get a card off to my mother on her birthday. First, I have the world's worst memory. Second, I never seem to have a card when I need one, and finally, if I have a card, I'm usually out of stamps. Is it okay for me to skip all this?

A I believe you might think about trying harder. Sending a few cards throughout the year is a small enough thing to do for a family to whom it obviously means so much.

The trick to sending cards, I think, is to be organized about it. Buy yourself one of the decorative calendars or books designed to remind you of birthdays and other special occasions. They're available in stationery and museum stores. The Metropolitan Museum in New York City has some particularly attractive books to help you remember birthdays and other occasions; their products are sold in other museums or can be ordered by mail.

If you have many dates to remember, it might be helpful to keep a three-by-five card file divided into the months. At the end of each month, check your file to see what cards you'll need for the upcoming month. Then purchase all your cards at once so they are on hand when you need them.

The post office is even lending forgetful people a hand these days. It is now possible to use a major credit card to order stamps through the mail or by telephone. They arrive in your mail a few days later.

We forgetful souls really don't have any excuses anymore.

Q I broke a wineglass at a friend's house the other night. I offered to replace it, but she said not to bother—that she has many more and expects one to break every now and then. What should I do?
A As a rule, when you break or damage something in someone's house, you should replace it, but since your friend has assured you that she does not want the glass replaced, you need not replace it. Do write your friend a note of apology, and if you want to, send her some flowers or a small gift in lieu of replacing her glass.

· Holiday Cards ·

Q After forty years of mailing more than 200 cards at Christmas, it is time to hone down my Christmas-card list. I haven't cut it in years, but I can no longer afford to send so many cards; nor am I able to write them all. How do I go about this? Do I tell people this is the last card they will receive from me?

A Begin by dropping all the people whom you have not heard from for a year or so. I would then drop those whom you consider to be acquaintances and/or purely business associates.

There is no need to make an announcement that you won't be sending any more cards to certain people. Most of us edit our Christmas-card lists from time to time; it is to be expected.

Q A friend's son committed suicide a few months ago, and I know she is still deeply mourning her loss. How can I possibly send her a Christmas card?

A People in mourning should never be ignored. They need all the kindness and attention they can get. Send your friend a Christmas card, but choose a card with a serious message rather than sending something gay or frivolous that is definitely not in keeping with her mood. Be sure to write a short personal message such as *Thinking of you.*

Q My niece recently married a Jewish man. My problem is this: My husband and I have always sent Christmas cards with a Christian religious message. Our cards are preprinted with our names. May I send them one of these cards?

A It would be more tactful to send a card with a more general holiday greeting rather than a specifically religious message. Individual cards are available at most stationery stores at holiday time, so you would not have to purchase an entire box.

Q I love sending Christmas cards, or holiday cards, as I prefer to think of them, since I always avoid buying cards with a distinctly "Christmas" message. I have always sent them to my Jewish friends, but one friend pointed out to me that this might actually be offensive, especially on the years when Chanukah is nowhere near the time of Christmas. Which of us is right?

A I'm with you. I love the custom of sending Christmas cards to good friends, and I, too, buy some cards that wish people *Happy Holidays* rather than saying *Merry Christmas.*

· I do continue to send my cards on or around Christmas even when Chanukah is early, because I think of them as New Year's cards, and the New Year always follows on the heels of Christmas.

Q I want to send Chanukah cards, but my mother, who is Orthodox and very traditional, says they are a Christian custom. What do you think?

A Chanukah cards are an outgrowth of the Christian custom of sending Christmas cards, but in a time when few of us maintain any kind of personal correspondence, I think they're a nice custom. Think of them as New Year's cards, and send them to those whom you know will enjoy them.

Q I have always sent Christmas cards—that is, cards with a distinctly religious message. I note that many of the cards I get in return do not even mention Christmas anymore. I think this misses the point of this very religious holiday. What is your opinion on this?

A Most people who send nonreligious cards—especially cards that do not mention Christmas—do so out of sensitivity toward their friends who are not religious or who perhaps are not even Christian. I personally applaud this spirit of ecumenicalism, although I understand your desire to keep Christmas as a religious holiday. Why don't you do what I and many other people do: Buy some cards with a religious message and some without.

· *Using the Telephone* ·

Q How do I instruct my housekeeper to answer my phone? She calls me by my first name, and I feel a little stuffy telling her to answer the phone, "Mrs. Berg's residence," even though I know that this is the correct way to do it.

A Just because your housekeeper calls you by your first name is no reason for her not to answer your phone properly. It will be easier for her and the person calling if she immediately makes it clear that she is not the woman of the house. She does this by answering the phone, "Mrs. Berg's residence" or "Berg residence."

Q At what age can my children begin answering the phone?
A When they're old enough to go to college? I'm obviously joking, but my point is serious: People let their children answer the telephone long before they should. Nothing is more annoying than trying to reach an adult friend and having to go through a small child's hoops to do so. I would like to remind all parents of small children that the telephone is neither a toy nor a learning device. Generally, I don't think children under the age of four or five should answer the telephone.

If you disagree and will permit yours to answer, then at least instruct them in how to do so. Teach them to say hello, wait for the caller to identify him- or herself, and then to put the person being called on the line without further ado.

Personal safety is another reason to keep small children away from the telephone. An indiscreet child may give out information you would not want given out.

Q How do I answer my own telephone at home?
A Simply say "Hello." One never answers one's own phone by saying, "Mrs. Morris's residence." Only employees and guests in a household answer the phone this way.

Q I work at home and during the course of a workday am called by both friends and business associates. How should I answer my telephone?

A I would answer it a little formally, more to suit your business associates than your friends. During business hours, you might answer the phone by saying, "Susan Alexander."

Q It seems like at least once a week our dinner is interrupted by a telephone solicitor. I don't want to be rude, but neither do I want to talk to these people while my food is getting cold—or at any other time, now that I think about it. What is the best way to handle these calls?

A Unfortunately, telephone solicitation is on the rise. I say unfortunately because I also dislike this form of selling. It invades a person's privacy—in his own home, no less. I believe in using a firm hand if you do not want to talk to someone who is trying to sell you something. Say, "I'm sorry, but I am not interested." Most telephone salespersons have been trained to be polite and to take no for an answer the first time, but if the person persists, you may feel justified in hanging up the telephone after repeating your message two or three times.

Lately, there seems to be a new twist, for when I have informed several callers that they have called at an inconvenient time, I have been asked when I would find a call convenient. I invariably reply, "At no time, really. I don't like telephone solicitation." While I believe in being civil, if enough of us make it clear that we are not open to this form of selling, maybe it will stop.

Q I'm offended when I call a friend's house and the person who answers wants to know who is calling. Must I answer?

A It is rude for someone to ask who is calling when a private home has been called, *but* it is ruder still for the caller not to identify him- or herself right away. When a telephone is answered, the caller should say, "Hello, this is Sally Wallace. May I speak with Marge, please?"

Q Must I tell someone's nosy secretary why I'm calling when I'm asked?"

A Generally, yes. As a matter of fact, you should identify yourself *before* you're asked. You need not share too many details, though. If you are returning a call, you may note that and say, "He'll know what I'm calling about." If you're a friend, you may say, "This is a personal call." Keep in mind that most secretaries have been instructed to ask who is calling, and that their bosses want to know before they come to the phone.

Q I have a friend who always puts me on the spot when she invites me to do something with her. Instead of inviting me somewhere, she asks me what I'm doing on a specific night. I don't have any room to wiggle out of the invitation if I want to. What's the best way to handle this type of situation?

A Many people are awkward with telephone invitations, although they don't mean to be. There is a right and a wrong way to extend a telephone invitation. For example:

- Never say, "What are you doing on such-and-such a night?" or "Are you busy . . ."
- Be direct. Say, "We're having people over for drinks on Tuesday night to watch the election returns and wondered if you would join us?"

In turn, there's also a polite way to respond to a telephone invitation:

- Answer immediately, if possible.
- If you cannot give an answer immediately, say, "I'll have to let you know." Always give an explanation of some sort so you don't sound as if you're simply waiting for a better invitation to come along.

Q I get a lot of wrong numbers and occasionally dial one myself. The people who call me usually hang up without saying anything, while I try to be polite. Am I overextending myself according to contemporary standards?

A You certainly are not. You shouldn't just hang up when you get a wrong number. Here's how to handle a wrong number when you dial one:

- Be polite.
- Don't ask the person you have called to tell you his or her number. Instead ask, "Have I dialed 222-8746?"
- If you call a friend inadvertently, identify yourself and offer some brief explanation.

Q My pet peeve is people who don't wait for me to answer my phone. I'm seventy-nine and don't move as fast as I used to. I need a few extra rings just to get to the phone.

A I couldn't agree more. Callers should let a phone ring at least ten times and even longer if they know the other person may need extra time to get to the phone.

Alternatively, those of you who wait for calls might want to take care not to answer regularly on the second or third ring because you will condition your callers to let your phone ring only a few times.

Q I have finally succumbed to a phone machine. On the one hand, I hate those cute messages so many people leave. On the other hand, I hate to have the only boring message in town. Any hints on what's polite?

A I'm afraid I fall on the side of boring. I don't like people to use their phone machines to entertain me. It just takes up time, and it's still impersonal. Furthermore, phone machines are so common that most people no longer need to be instructed in how to leave a message.

I like a straightforward message that says something like this: "Hello, you have reached Joan Simpson. If you would like to leave a message, please do so after you hear the beep." If you absolutely must know when a call came in, add: "Please also leave the date and time you called." If you don't really need this information, then don't ask for it.

There is also an obligation on the side of those who leave messages. Keep them short and to the point. Don't conduct an entire conversation on the telephone. Do tell someone when his or her machine seems not to be working.

8

. . . .

CEREMONIES AND CELEBRATIONS

· Showers ·

Q I'm giving a baby shower for a friend. She's a very friendly person and knows almost everyone in our neighborhood. She's not sure whom to invite and doesn't want any hurt feelings over this. What would you suggest?

A She should supply you with a guest list. Since the invitation obligates the recipient to give a gift, a good rule of thumb is for her to invite anyone whose shower she would like to attend—and whom she would be pleased to buy a gift for.

Q I'm giving a wedding shower for a cousin. We'll invite our relatives, of course, but beyond that, she doesn't know whom to ask. Should she ask her work colleagues? She's not equally friendly with everyone, but she works in a small office so she's reluctant to invite some people and not everyone.

A Your cousin might do well to make this shower for family and purely social friends. If she's very close to one or two persons at work, she could invite them and ask them to be discreet since she is not inviting everyone from the office. I have a hunch that the office crew will give her a shower, too, and that will make everyone happy.

Q I've volunteered to give a baby shower for a friend, but I've never given a shower before. What do I do?
A Showers are wonderfully happy parties, and they're lots of fun to plan.

First, think about the timing. Most baby showers are given during a woman's seventh or eighth month of pregnancy. Waiting until the seventh month pretty much ensures that nothing will go wrong, and waiting until the ninth month is risky, because the guest of honor may find herself otherwise occupied at the last minute.

Surprise showers are not unusual, but if you decide to do this, do your friend a favor and arrange the surprise so that she has a chance to look her best. Many women feel unattractive and ungainly in the last months of pregnancy, and it's no favor to catch a friend completely off-guard under these circumstances. You want your guest of honor to shine.

Next, choose a color scheme. Yellow is an obvious one, as are pink and blue, but you might also use green, peach, or lavender—whatever appeals to you and looks pretty.

Baby showers are not usually theme-oriented the way bridal showers are. By that I mean you don't give a clothes shower or an equipment shower, but rather, you let people bring whatever gifts they like. Guests often do check in with you, and you can keep track of what people are giving to avoid duplicates. If asked, you may suggest items you know the mother-to-be needs.

Lunchtime or early afternoon are the usual times for baby showers, although these days, they are sometimes held during the evening hours.

People will gather at the appointed time, and you should have something for them to nibble on. When everyone has had time to socialize, the guest of honor opens gifts. Often she does this sitting in a specially decorated chair. Afterward, a meal is usually served, followed by dessert and coffee. Sometimes the meal is served, gifts are opened, and then coffee and dessert are served. The guest of honor for a shower usually stays until the end to say good-bye to her friends.

Thank-you notes should be written for any presents from absentee guests, and the guest of honor should call the hostess to thank her for the party.

· *Christening* ·

Q   I want to have a home christening for my baby. How do I arrange for this?

A   Begin by contacting the clergyperson to set a date. He or she can give you specific guidelines, but in general here is what you do:

- Select a location, usually either the dining room or the living room. Arrange for a small silver bowl, which will hold the baptismal water, to be placed on a high table. You may want to surround it with flowers and also have a pretty bouquet or two around the room.
- Chairs are not set up for the guests, who are composed of the family and close friends, but if grandparents or great-grandparents would be more comfortable seated, chairs may be placed near the temporary font for them.
- Guests arrive and mingle, although drinks are not usually served and not much time elapses between the arrival hour and the ceremony. The mother and baby may greet guests, or they may remain in seclusion in another room.
- At the agreed-upon time, the clergyperson dons his or her robe and enters the room, followed by the parents and godparents. The godparents carry the baby. If there are no godparents, the parents carry the baby.

- Close relatives stand near the front, and friends stand behind them.
- The ceremony, which takes only a few minutes, is performed, after which everyone gathers around to offer congratulations and ogle the baby.
- A punch is traditionally served, but more often these days, champagne is poured, and everyone drinks to the baby's health and happiness. The other traditional food is a white cake. A luncheon is sometimes served.

All of the celebrating usually takes place without the little guest of honor—who, one hopes, has been returned to the nursery for an afternoon nap.

Q I've given a friend's baby a shower present, and I took a gift to the hospital. Must I also give a christening gift?
A You may give a gift if you want to, but you need not, especially if you live on a limited income. Alternatively, you might take a small bouquet or some token present.

Next time, if you know you will be invited to a christening, take flowers to the baby's mother in the hospital and save the present for the christening.

Q We want to ask some good friends to be our son's godparents, but we're afraid we'll hurt my sister and her husband's feelings if we do so. Can you help us?
A Usually, family members are not asked to be godparents, the thought being that the baby's family is expanded by honorary relatives.

There also may be some religious restrictions upon whom you can choose. Some religions require that godparents be of the same religion as the child.

Godparents are honorary, and their primary obligation to the child is spiritual. They are charged with overseeing the child's religious upbringing, although it would be virtually unheard of for them actually to interfere. Their larger, more ceremonial, role is to be a special friend to the child, someone who remembers birthdays and other special occasions.

Q We are planning our baby's christening. What kind of invitations should we send and whom should we include on the guest list?
A Invitations to a christening are usually made by telephone, with notes sent to any out-of-town guests. A christening is usually a small celebration, a gathering of close family and friends. It is never used to repay invitations of any kind.

Q What kind of clothes should I wear to my daughter's christening, which will take place at home? What should my guests wear?
A Since this is a religious ceremony, whether it takes place at home or in a church, you and your guests should wear clothes you would wear to church. Neither the mother nor the godmother should wear black on this joyous occasion.

Q What kind of outfit is appropriate for my son to wear at his christening? I always envisioned a long, lacy white dress, but I'm not sure anyone really wears them, and my husband objects to putting a boy in anything so frilly.
A Yes, such dresses are worn by both boys and girls; they are, in fact, often handed down through families. You can purchase a new one in any good baby-clothing store or department store. If your husband seriously objects, however, why not think about putting some other good white outfit on your baby? The more important—and traditional—thing, I think, is that he wear white.

Q What time of day is a christening held?
A If the christening is held during the regular worship service,

it will be in the morning, sometime between 9:00 A.M. and noon. A home christening usually takes place around noon or in the early afternoon.

Q When—that is, how soon after birth—is a christening scheduled?
A This depends upon the religion. The Roman Catholic Church used to christen babies within days of their birth, which often meant the mother could not be present. They now wait until the mother can attend but still prefer to do a christening in the first few weeks of a baby's life. Protestants christen in the first two to six months, although some denominations wait until the child is several years old, and some baptize only adults.

Q We were godparents for a friend's baby ten years ago, but we have since moved several times and have, I'm sorry to say, lost touch with the family. Am I at fault for not maintaining the tie, and should I do anything?
A There is no need to worry about this if the ties have been broken. This is not an unusual situation in today's mobile world.

· Bris/Naming Ceremony ·

Q We know we will be having a boy next month and have begun to think about the bris and the celebration that goes with it. How do we plan it?
A A bris, also called a *berith* or *Brith Milah,* is the circumcision ceremony for a Jewish male. It is held on the eighth day of the infant's life, unless there is a medical reason to do it later.

Some hospitals have facilities for doing circumcisions, but most parents prefer to do it in their home and to accompany it with a celebration.

The ceremony, which is performed by a rabbi or a man specially trained to do circumcisions (a *mohel*), is usually done in the morning or early afternoon. Lunch or brunch is customarily served. It is often catered, coming as it does so soon after the baby's birth.

Q   Who is invited to a bris?
A   Family and close friends are invited to a bris. Invitations are, of necessity, issued by telephone.

Q   How do I arrange a bris?
A   Call your rabbi to notify him or her of the birth. The rabbi will either do the circumcision or arrange for a *mohel* to do it. If a *mohel* does it, the rabbi may not be present.
    A male—often a relative but sometimes a family friend—is selected to be the *sandek*, a godparent who holds the child during the ceremony. Other honorary roles exist for family and friends. Someone may be given the honor of carrying the baby into the room. The baby may be passed through the arms of several friends and relatives as he is carried to the table where the circumcision is done. Often these are young couples who are themselves hoping to have children.

Q   What kind of present do I take to a bris?
A   Close relatives often give larger or more lasting gifts, and friends bring whatever baby gift they would ordinarily give the baby.

Q   What do I wear to a bris?
A   Dress as you would for any religious service. Hats or yarmulkes are worn by men and also by women in the Conservative and Orthodox denominations.

Q   We have been invited to a naming ceremony. What is this and what is expected of us?
A   This is a ceremony for a Jewish girl in which she is formally

named in the temple on the Sabbath closest to the thirtieth day of her birth. In the past, no celebration has accompanied this ceremony, but today parents are beginning to plan a celebration similar to that accompanying a bris. Since the naming ceremony takes place in a temple, the celebration may be held there, or a home reception may follow. Presents are given to the baby.

· First Communion ·

Q   A friend's child will be taking First Communion shortly, and I am invited back to her house for the reception. I'm not Catholic, so I'm not sure what is expected.

A   I like the ecumenicalism that I increasingly see these days among friends of different religions. A First Communion is an important day in a Roman Catholic child's life, one that he or she will have prepared for over several months. It occurs when the child is seven or eight.

Whether you attend the church service or just the reception held later at the parents' home, dress as you would for any church service.

A present for the youngster is called for. If you are a close relative, you will want to get something of special or lasting value—a rosary, bible, or prayer book, for example. Money is also a traditional gift in many families. The only thing you should *not* do is give the child a frivolous gift on such an important religious day for him or her.

Q   My daughter is going to take her First Communion soon. The school has issued guidelines for dress, but they have said only that girls should wear white. I wore something that was like a miniature wedding dress, complete with a veil, for my First Communion. Is this appropriate today?

A   In some communities, little girls are dressed in elaborate white dresses with veils, but in others, they wear a simpler white dress. Appropriate dress for boys consists of a gray or blue suit, or jacket with shorts, a white shirt, and a tie. Sometimes just a white shirt and nice pants are worn. Schools or churches usually issue guidelines for dress, or you can check with the other parents to see what their children are wearing.

· Confirmation/Bar Mitzvah ·

Q My son is going to be confirmed. I was not brought up in a religious family, so I'm not sure what is expected on this occasion.
A Roman Catholics confirm youngsters, or take them into the congregation officially, at age eleven or twelve; Protestants, a year or two later. A separate service is held for Catholics; Protestants incorporate confirmation into the regular church service. Some Jewish Reform congregations confirm their members rather than having a bar mitzvah.

A reception is usually held at the church or synagogue, but parents can also plan a family gathering at their home. A light lunch or buffet meal is usually served.

Q What should my daughter wear for her confirmation in a Protestant church?
A Girls may be requested to wear white. If not, they should wear a pretty dress suitable for church. Boys wear dark suits, usually with long pants, white shirts, and ties. On a very hot day, or if the congregation dresses informally, the jacket could be omitted.

Q My husband and I, who are Protestant, are invited to a bar mitzvah service. What is expected of us? What will happen?
A A bar mitzvah (or, in the case of a girl, the bat mitzvah) is

a coming-of-age ceremony for a Jewish child. Like the Protestant confirmation ceremony, it marks his or her acceptance as an adult member of the congregation. The child will have studied for up to a year or more and learned at least some Hebrew for the occasion.

The ceremony often takes place on the Sabbath at the Saturday morning service, but it can be held on any day that the Torah is read. A reception, or *kiddish*, featuring bread and wine, may be held immediately afterward in the temple for the entire congregation.

Dress as you would for any religious service. If the temple is Conservative or Orthodox, women may wear hats; you can check with your hostess. Jewish men typically cover their heads for religious services. Yarmulkes will be provided in the foyer to the sanctuary.

Q We are planning our son's bar mitzvah. The temple we belong to has urged us to keep the celebration low-key, but our family will expect a big, elaborate party. Can you suggest anything?
A A private party for family and friends usually follows the bar mitzvah service. This may range from a party that is every bit the equal of a formal wedding, complete with a dance band, to a much less elaborate luncheon held after the service. I think you should have the kind of party that pleases you—and your son.

I have friends who were faced with your dilemma. They went ahead with a more modest lunch than their families expected but injected it with so many warm touches, including a klezmer band, that everyone had an absolutely great time.

· Birthdays ·

Q My seven-year-old has been invited to several wonderful birthday parties planned around special themes, and now he wants to have one. I'd like to do something really creative, but I'm not sure how to go about it. Any hints?

A Youngsters this age like circuses and magic, just to get you started. If your child has any special interest, such as dinosaurs, baseball (or any other sport), outer space, or ballet, why not plan a party around this? Do whatever you can to carry out the theme. Decorate the party room appropriately, have a "theme" cake made, buy favors that tie in with the theme, and even plan games that are theme-oriented.

Don't overlook the possibility of moving a theme party out of your home and incorporating some activity, such as swimming, visiting a zoo or farm, attending a children's performance, or going to a special museum. Some museums, such as the Museum of Natural History in New York City, have preplanned birthday packages based on special themes (dinosaurs is a current one), or sometimes you can take a group of youngsters to an already-scheduled activity. If your local museum doesn't have a party package, perhaps you could suggest one for them.

Q I want to have a birthday party for my five-year-old, but here's my problem. He already has an active social life and has gone to several very elaborate parties where professional entertainers amused the children. I don't believe in doing things on so grandiose a scale for small children, but I don't want to look like a miser. Any suggestions?

A Yes, I agree with you that children's birthday parties have become rather competitive these days, with parents vying to see who can spend the most money on children who would be perfectly happy with something far less elaborate. Don't worry about being a miser; just stick with your values and plan a party on a scale that you find acceptable.

Most children this age like very simple food—cake and ice cream, in fact, will do just fine. I do like the custom of giving party favors, if only because it teaches the birthday child that he or she must give as well as receive.

There's also an old Jewish custom that everyone could institute: Children are weighed on each birthday, and a sum equal to the child's change in weight is donated to charity. You might even engage your child in selecting the group or person to whom he would like to give the money.

Q   I live in a small apartment, but my twelve-year-old is insisting that she wants a birthday party. Any ideas on how to carry this off?

A   Yes, plan something away from your home—a movie, the theater, or a skating party, for example, or a trip to an amusement park or some other special destination.

Q   A friend and I are having an argument. I say that thank-you notes are not necessary for birthday presents given to a child who is too young to write them. She says the parent must write them on the child's behalf. Who is right?

A   Sorry, but your friend wins this one hands down. A thank you must be sent, written either by the child who received the gift or by a parent. I would encourage children to write them as soon as they are able, however, just so they get used to this custom.

Q   When is it appropriate to have a birthday party for an adult? My husband will be forty next month, and I would like to plan a big surprise party for him.

A   While adults don't regularly have birthday parties, they are great ideas for what I like to call the "big birthdays." My only word of caution is to be sure your husband will enjoy a surprise party. People don't always mean it when they say they don't want a party, but they usually mean it when they say they don't want a surprise party.

· Graduation ·

Q My daughter is graduating from high school next month. What kind of party should I plan?

A It is usual to give a party for a high-school graduation, while college and graduate-school degrees are typically celebrated on a much smaller scale, usually with a family dinner or a small present.

For the high-school graduation party, send printed or written invitations to family and friends. It's customary to invite the graduate's friends (even though many of them will be occupied with their own graduation parties at the same time) as well as family and your own friends. You may include a response card if you feel it is necessary.

Any kind of party is okay—a pool party, a barbecue, picnic, buffet, or brunch. Decorations are usually kept simple, but there is no reason not to go all out with a theme party if you choose to do so.

Q My son is graduating from high school. I have just learned that he is entitled to only four invitations for the ceremony. His father and I, a sister and brother, and four grandparents all expect to attend. What do I do?

A Yours is not an unusual situation. Most high schools, of necessity, limit the invitations to about this number. Be grateful that your son has only two siblings. You have, it seems to me, a very neat situation at hand. You and your other children will attend.

If your child's siblings are away at school, or are willing to give up their seats, then you must decide among the grandparents. Some people draw names out of a hat; others invite no one so as not to hurt anyone. One thing I do know: Such situations are a good reason to give a party and make that the real celebration.

Q My daughter is going through the graduation ceremony with her class in June, but she really has one more class to complete and will not receive her diploma until January. When should I plan a party for her?

A The party should be held in January when she truly graduates.

Q To whom do I send graduation announcements?

A In the days when they imposed no obligation to send a gift, graduation announcements were sent to all friends and acquaintances. Today, the trend is toward more rather than less gift giving, and a graduation announcement is now seen as carrying an obligation for a gift. Therefore, send them only to close friends and relatives who will want to send a gift in any event. Alternatively, you might write on the invitation, "Just wanted to let you know the good news" and hope that the recipient will read between the lines and realize that a present is not necessary.

Announcements are often printed, and schools usually provide them for students or make arrangements for students to buy them at a special price.

Q How should I handle opening presents at my daughter's graduation? I know that some people, mostly family, will bring them while others may not. Should she still open gifts in front of everyone?

A Relatives do usually bring gifts to the graduation party. Gifts are not obligatory at a big party, but anyone who wants to may give one.

Presents should not be opened at a big party when some guests will have brought a gift and some will not.

· Anniversaries ·

Q My husband and I are approaching our fortieth wedding anniversary. We are thinking of giving a dinner dance for the occasion. Is it proper for us to give our own party? Is it proper to do so for our fortieth?

A Yes and yes. The most celebrated anniversaries are the twenty-fifth and the fiftieth, but you may ask your friends to join you for any anniversary you wish. When you give the party for yourselves, the occasion is usually not mentioned on the invitation. Your friends and close family will know what the party is all about, and everyone else will learn this when they arrive, but you won't have been put in the position of asking people to give you presents.

Q Our children insist on having a big party for our fiftieth anniversary. My husband and I aren't sure we're up to it, and we hate to have our children go to so much expense. Can't we say no?

A Children often give parties for their parents' major anniversaries—that is, for their twenty-fifth, or silver, and fiftieth, or golden, anniversaries. I suggest that you simply sit back and enjoy yourselves since you won't have to do any of the work. If you really feel you are not up to anything very fancy, discuss this with your children and ask them to scale down the celebration to something you can handle.

Keep in mind, though, that several things can be done to make the event less of a strain on you. For example, you need not stand on a receiving line. The more usual way to organize a fiftieth-anniversary receiving line is for the couple to sit to greet their guests. The party can be held in the afternoon or planned as a luncheon if that will be easier on you. You may even suggest whom you would like to see invited—another way to control the size of the party.

Q We want to give an anniversary party for our parents golden wedding anniversary but aren't sure what to do. Could you give us some hints?

A You may give as informal or formal a party as you like,

meaning that it may be a casual buffet or a four-course, black-tie dinner party with full orchestra.

Do keep in mind as you plan the party what your parents are able to handle. If they have been married for fifty years, they aren't spring chickens any longer (see the preceding letter for the other side of the story).

The party may be held in a home, a club, or a rented hall. Sometimes when a couple wish to reaffirm their vows, they hold a reception in a church or temple.

Q We're sending printed invitations to our parents' twenty-fifth wedding anniversary. Our parents don't really need anything, but we would like to send them on a special trip. Would it be all right to ask our guests to contribute to a fund for the trip rather than bringing presents?
A It's not gracious to ask your guests to give money or anything else. You should arrange for the trip among yourselves and then present it to your parents at the party.

Q We recently received an invitation to an anniversary party for friends. The invitation read: *In lieu of a gift, please send a donation that will help to buy a memento of the occasion.* What do you think of this?
A It is an out-and-out solicitation for a gift, and that is always rude. I suggest you ignore the suggestion and buy your friends whatever present you would like.

Q Is it correct to write *No gifts please* on an anniversary invitation for our parents? My parents insist that they do not want any presents.
A You may write this, and their close friends will probably still choose to ignore it.

9

. . . .

WEDDINGS

· Engagements ·

Q What is an acceptable length for an engagement?
A There is no "acceptable" length for an engagement. How long you are engaged depends upon the circumstances surrounding your engagement and your future plans. Most engaged couples want to marry as quickly as possible, so the average engagement is about five months. There is usually a reason behind a longer engagement: Several months' notice may be needed to engage a room; one or both of you may be finishing school; or one of you may be in the military or temporarily living in another community.

Q I am about to get engaged to a wonderful man whom my family has never met. I suppose this is not so unusual, given that we live 750 miles apart. But it still feels awkward to go home with a man to whom I'm already engaged. Is this correct?
A You're right in assuming that your situation is not unusual

these days. Still, there are some things you can do to ease the way. If you haven't begun preparing your family for your imminent good news, do so immediately. In telephone calls and letters, let them know there is someone special in your life. You could even hold off on announcing your engagement formally until your parents have met your fiancé. But there is nothing wrong with getting engaged to someone before your family meets him—provided you take him home at the earliest opportunity to meet your family.

Q   Whom do we announce our engagement to first—my family or my fiancé's family?
A   Back in the days when a man actually asked a woman's family for her hand in marriage, the good news was always broken first to her family. Today, most couples try to break it to each family on the same day—and it really doesn't matter who is called first. If both sets of parents know that an engagement is about to be announced, you might even get them together—over brunch or dinner—to break the news "officially."

Q   How do our parents get together now that we're engaged?
A   Not too long ago, it was mandatory that the parents of the groom call on the bride's family. Formal calls are now a thing of the past, and many people don't know about this sticky little rule of etiquette.
   It really doesn't matter who calls on whom; what matters is that the two sets of parents meet. If the bride's mother does not hear from the groom's mother within a couple of weeks after the engagement is announced, she should write or telephone them.
   These days, when the two families may live thousands of miles apart, they may not even meet until shortly before the wedding takes place.

Q I am about to become engaged and will meet my prospective bride's parents for the first time when we tell them. I am embarrassed about having been married twice before. My future bride knows about my past, but need I discuss it with her parents?
A Yes, you must mention your previous marriages to them. While the man no longer formally asks for a woman's hand in marriage, problems involving money, health, previous marriages, children, and religious differences should be acknowledged and discussed with your fiancée and her parents. They are entitled to hear these things from you or her and not from a stranger.

Q I'm about to get engaged. We have chosen a ring and set a date. We have only one small problem. I am still married to my previous husband and will be until about two weeks before my wedding. May I wear my new engagement ring anyway?
A It would be in extremely poor taste for you to wear one man's engagement ring while still married to another man. I understand that divorces are often long and drawn out, or even that some people quickly rebound from a bad marriage to marry again. If you plan a small, quiet wedding, I see no problem with your marrying shortly after your divorce, but I don't think you can wear the engagement ring until you are officially divorced— even if that happens twenty minutes before your wedding.

Q Must I get a diamond engagement ring even though I'd rather have another stone? Is it bad luck not to wear a diamond?
A The custom of wearing a diamond engagement ring has little to do with luck and everything to do with hype. A few decades ago, diamonds were promoted as *the* engagement stone, and now almost every woman who gets an engagement ring gets a diamond. But almost any stone is suitable, and these days, many other precious stones are rarer than diamonds anyway. Many women opt for their birthstone, which may be either a precious

or semiprecious stone, and some choose rings set with other precious stones such as rubies, emeralds, or sapphires.

Since you mentioned luck, I will tell you that the wearing of opals is considered bad luck unless they are your birthstone.

Q I want to buy my fiancée an engagement ring but have a limited budget. What can I do?
A Visit your local jeweler alone to discuss your needs and price range. He or she can then show you an assortment of rings and stones in your price range from which you can choose a selection. When you return with your fiancée to make the final selection, she will be shown the rings and stones you have selected.

Q I wear very little jewelry and don't want an engagement ring. Is this okay? How do I explain it to people?
A It is perfectly acceptable to become engaged without a ring, and you should not have to explain it to anyone.

Q I am a widow who is about to become engaged. Since my husband's death, I have worn my wedding and engagement rings. What do I do with them now?
A When you become engaged, if not before, you should remove your engagement and wedding rings. You may do one of two things with them: Either keep them as heirloom gifts for your children or have the stones reset into another piece of jewelry, which you can either continue to wear or pass on to a child.

Q My fiancé recently broke off our engagement after two years of our seeing each other and one year of being engaged. He wants me to return the ring. I say he has caused me enough aggravation, and the ring is my consolation prize. But I've agreed to let you settle this.

A You may be sorry you decided to make me the judge, because I think you should return the ring, along with any heirloom jewelry he gave you.

And although you didn't ask, I should tell you that any engagement gifts from friends and relatives should also be returned, along with a brief note explaining that since the wedding has been cancelled, you no longer feel right about keeping the gifts. The only exception is monogrammed presents, which obviously are of no use to anyone except you.

· Showers ·

Q My half sister would like to give a shower for me, but I've read that close family members do not give showers. Is that true?
A That's right. Anyone may give a shower *except* the immediate family—which includes mothers, sisters (even half sisters), grandmothers, and mothers- and grandmothers-in-law.

I admit that there are occasions—such as when the bride has never lived in the community of the groom's family—when the groom's family may wish to pave the way for her. At most, the mother of the groom or one of his sisters may hint to a close family friend that a shower would be most appreciated. Someone might say to a close friend: "I feel bad that I can't give Sukhreet a shower, even though she's coming all the way from India to marry John." This is a gentle kind of hint, which a friend may feel free to ignore or to respond to, if it is convenient for her to do so. The groom's family may, of course, have a party to introduce Sukhreet to their friends, but they may not solicit gifts.

Q A friend has kindly offered to give me a bridal shower, but I'm not sure whom I should invite.
A Showers, which used to be fairly intimate affairs that in-

cluded the bride's and groom's close female relatives and friends, now often have large guest lists of thirty or more. You must decide which kind of shower you prefer. Keep in mind that you can't invite anyone to a shower whom you don't intend to invite to the wedding and that, except for your mothers, sisters, and members of the wedding party, no one should be invited to more than one shower. Those who are invited to more than one shower should be told to skip the gift after the first party. They may still bring a small, token present, but that is up to them.

A good rule of thumb is to invite anyone whom you would be delighted to buy a present for should the situation be reversed.

Q I am about to marry for the second time although, unlike my first wedding, this wedding will be low-key and quiet. My question is this: May I permit a friend to give a shower for me, given that this is my second wedding?

A In general, I see no reason why you should not have a shower for this wedding, but your decision should be based on several factors. One is how large your last wedding was and, more important, how long ago it was. If you married at a large, lavish wedding only a year ago, you might have second thoughts about another shower, not least because people will wonder what you could possibly need in the way of household gifts. If several years have elapsed and, as is often the case, you have many new friends, then I don't see why you shouldn't have a shower to which you invite close friends. I don't think a large shower that includes much of the guest list from the first wedding would be appropriate for anyone who is remarrying.

Q I have just been invited to a shower for a distant cousin who lives in another city. I am not even planning to attend the wedding. Am I obligated to send a wedding present and a shower present? I'm afraid I live on a strict budget.

A   This is my idea of a shower guest list gone awry. You should not have received an invitation to this shower and need not feel obligated to send a shower gift. For that matter, you need not send a wedding gift if you are not attending the wedding—that is, unless you truly want to.

Q   May I register for wedding gifts at more than one store?

A   Yes, many couples register their preferences at a department store and then also register at a specialty store.

Q   This is my second wedding. Must I—or may I—register for gifts?

A   There is no hard-and-fast rule about this. If your first wedding was small and took place several years ago, you may register if you really want to. Most couples do not register for a second wedding, in part because it is assumed that the bride received— and after her divorce, kept—many basic household items at the time of her first wedding. If this is the groom's second wedding, and the bride has never been married before, then everything goes off as if this were a first wedding and you may, of course, register.

Q   I am invited to a wedding and am unsure whether to take the gift or send it. I usually take my present to the wedding, but someone told me this isn't the right way to do it. Is this true?

A   What's right varies from community to community. At some weddings, people bring gifts to the wedding. At others, and especially if the gift is coming from out of town, it is better—and easier—to send it. In most cases, a gift can be sent from the store where it is purchased.

Q A good friend of mine is getting remarried. I understand that I need not give a gift for a second marriage, but I want to. My question is this: Will other guests, who are not giving gifts, be embarrassed if I bring the gift to the wedding? Should I send it ahead of time to the bride?

A I think gifts are just fine at second—and even third—weddings. After all, our best wishes for the success of the marriage are just the same for each one. You may send the gift or take it to the wedding. The bride and groom won't open it at the wedding, anyway.

Q I have very unusual taste, and most people say they never know whether a gift will be right for me or not. Would it be okay to add a line to my wedding invitation saying that money would be appreciated?

A No. This would be in extremely bad taste.

Q When is it appropriate for a couple to give a joint wedding gift?

A A joint gift may be given by an engaged couple or an unmarried couple who live together or who have gone together long enough to be known as a couple. When a friend who is not part of a regular couple is invited and told she or he may bring a date, she, for example, usually gives a present that is from her alone. Her name is signed to the card and she pays for the present.

Q Must I open gifts that are brought to my wedding?

A No, you should not open gifts that are brought to the wedding. If you anticipate that many people will bring presents, and this seems to be a custom that is gaining in popularity, set up a table on which to put the gifts. It need not be decorated, but it may need to be covered with a cloth. Make arrangements in advance for someone to remove the wedding gifts after the wedding.

Q Is it okay to exchange a particularly atrocious present? A great-aunt is known for her eccentric gifts, and I know she is going to give me an expensive, one-of-a-kind piece of porcelain that I will hate.

A The good news is that wedding gifts that are duplicates may be exchanged. The bad news is that you should not exchange a one-of-a-kind gift if there is any possibility that the person who gave it to you will ever visit. Sorry, but I'm sure you can see the consequences—and hurt feelings—that would arise. No one intentionally gives an unattractive gift. And everyone is flattered to see a gift they have given someone displayed—at least for the duration of the visit.

Q How long may I take to write thank-you notes after my wedding? I have a job that requires many extra hours, and I'm having a big wedding, so I will receive lots of presents.

A Three months is the longest you should take to write thank-you notes, which, by the way, must be handwritten and should make a direct reference to the present.

It will help if you can keep up with writing thank-you notes as the gifts arrive before the wedding. If you absolutely cannot answer them within this amount of time, you might send printed announcements that read:

> Mr. and Mrs. John Smith
> gratefully acknowledge
> your present
> and will respond personally
> at the earliest opportunity.

Alternatively, have you thought about sharing the responsibility with your husband? There is no reason that your groom could not write some of the thank-you notes.

Q Am I obligated to send a gift if I don't go to a wedding?
A Strictly speaking, no, but many people do, especially if they are relatives or close friends of the bride and/or groom who simply cannot make the trip because of the distance involved.

· *The Reception* ·

Q Must I have a wedding reception? The only time our minister can marry us is at 5 P.M. on a Saturday, and we need to catch a plane to Europe at 10 P.M.
A No, you need not have a reception, although it is very rare these days not to have one, and it may seem a little rude if there are out-of-towners at the wedding. Perhaps your parents would be willing to entertain them anyway, even if you can't attend the reception for very long.

When there is no reception, you should greet your wedding guests at the back of the church as they exit the sanctuary.

Q In my church, the minister invites everyone in the congregation to every wedding. My question is this: Do I have to invite everyone to my reception?
A Your situation is similar to that in some small towns where the local custom is to issue a general invitation in the newspaper engagement announcement. Unless local custom in your church dictates that you invite everyone, you need not invite people who respond to the public invitation, unless you want to.

Q My parents, who have been divorced for fifteen years, still aren't friendly. My mother doesn't want my father to come to the reception she is giving for my wedding, and he insists that he will give me another reception. Have you ever heard of this? Who gets invited to each reception? Also, should I wear my wedding dress to each reception?

A It is not unheard of for a couple to have two receptions. Sometimes one is held in each of their hometowns. In your case, one reception, probably your mother's, will be held immediately following the wedding, and those who are invited to the wedding will attend it.

Your father's reception can be held later the same day or after you return from your honeymoon. Your father's reception will be attended by his friends and relatives, whereas your mother's will be attended by her friends and relatives. Your friends may attend either one.

If both receptions are held on the same day, presumably one will be in the late morning or afternoon, and the other will be held at night. For variety, the evening festivities might be more formal than the afternoon ones, and you might plan dancing. Try to allow a few hours between parties so you and your wedding party can rest up.

If the second reception is held on the same day as the first one, you and your wedding party would wear your wedding clothes. If it is held on a later day, you may wear your wedding dress, but your attendants would not wear their wedding clothes. I hope you enjoy your parties. In my book, there is no such thing as too many wedding festivities!

Q I can't afford a large wedding reception. My fiancé and I are paying for everything. Do you have any suggestions for us?

A There are three key things you can do to keep reception costs down. The first is to limit the guest list. The second is to limit the food and liquor costs. And the third is to limit the decorations.

Limiting the guest list is the biggest problem for many people, especially those with large families and many friends. What's more, if people have traveled very far to attend your wedding, then you owe them nourishment and entertainment.

Some brides plan a simple church reception for everyone who

comes to the wedding and a smaller dinner afterward for a much more limited group of family and friends.

The kind of food you serve is dictated by the time of day you hold your reception. If you have a morning wedding, you will have to serve breakfast, but it's a relatively inexpensive meal. If you marry in the late morning or around noon, you should serve lunch, which is also inexpensive but is usually more expensive than breakfast. If you have an evening reception, then you will have to serve dinner, and that is the most expensive meal of all.

Best of all in terms of keeping down the cost is an afternoon reception, where you can basically offer dessert and punch, plus a few accompaniments. Keep in mind that a buffet or cocktail menu will also be less expensive than a sit-down dinner.

Liquor is another major expense that can be controlled. The most expensive option is to have an open bar with mixed drinks; the least expensive is to have alcoholic punch and coffee and tea. Both are perfectly acceptable.

Finally, if you are on a budget, keep the decorations simple. Plan fewer flowers or buy less-expensive arrangements. Greens tied with pretty ribbons make a lovely, inexpensive arrangement. Or buy your flowers wholesale and arrange them yourself. Sometimes you can use the altar flowers at the reception. Remember that the cheapest flowers are those that are in season.

Q   Must I serve a meal at my wedding reception?
A   Whether or not you serve a meal depends upon the hour of your reception (see the preceding letter) and local custom in your community. Among some groups, it would be unheard of to have a wedding and not serve a meal. Jewish custom, for example, dictates that a meal accompany all happy, festive occasions.

Q   I hate receiving lines. Can I skip this at my wedding?
A   Why would you want to skip the one receiving line where

you will be the star? I think I can safely promise you they are more fun to be in than to go through.

I don't think you should skip the receiving line for another reason: It is a chance for you to introduce your new husband and for him to introduce you, as well as an opportunity to thank people for coming to the wedding.

Q Who stands in the receiving line? My parents are divorced, and I don't think they will want to stand together.
A Don't worry, the fathers of the bride and groom may circulate among the guests rather than standing in the receiving line. The order of the receiving line is as follows: mother of the bride, father of the groom (optional), mother of the groom, father of the bride (optional), bride, groom, maid (or matron) of honor, bridesmaids. The groomsmen don't stand in the receiving line.

Q I am going to a wedding soon and would like to skirt the receiving line. I never know what to say to people. Any advice?
A Receiving lines aren't difficult to handle, mostly because no one expects much from you in the way of conversation. Tell the mothers how lovely you thought the wedding was. Tell the bride how beautiful she looks. Tell the groom how lucky he is. Tell the bridesmaids how beautiful they look. And you're done.

Q I was brought up to think that one never congratulates a bride but instead wishes her well. Someone told me this is old-fashioned. What do you think?
A These days you may congratulate both the bride and groom. "Best wishes" was always an awkward phrase, and no one misses it. It arose in the days when it was considered an insult to imply that any blushing bride had somehow snared her husband and was to be congratulated for the effort.

Q Who sits at the bride's table? I think my parents should be there since they're giving me my wedding, but my sister insists that the wedding party sits there.

A These days the trend is toward smaller, rather than long, banquetlike tables. When seating is limited, the bride and groom and their attendants sit together. The bride's and groom's parents sit together at another table, often with grandparents or other close relatives or friends. If you have room, you could seat both sets of parents with you, but basically, your sister is right. They do not ordinarily sit with you.

Q I have just been informed by my future sister-in-law that her family likes to sit together at weddings, not with the other family. Is this acceptable?

A I'm not fond of this custom of seating the two families at separate tables. On this one day, if no other, the parents of the bride and the parents of the groom should be seated together to share in the joint happiness of their two children.

· The Wedding ·

Q I have always dreamed of a wedding dress with a long train and veil. But I'm having an afternoon wedding for sixty people, and I'm wondering if this kind of dress will be too formal for the occasion.

A There are varying degrees of formality for weddings, which dictate dress and the size of the guest list (larger weddings are more formal than small ones).

For the most formal daytime and evening weddings, the bride wears a long white dress, train, and veil. For a semiformal daytime and evening wedding, she wears a long white, trainless dress and a short veil, short being anywhere from face to waist length. For an informal daytime wedding, she wears a short cocktail dress or suit, and for evening she wears a long dinner dress or short cocktail dress. She may wear a cocktail hat, usually with a small veil, or nothing at all. The wedding party always dresses with the same degree of formality as the bride.

You are planning an informal wedding and want to wear a formal wedding dress. You can do one of two things: Settle for a dress with a veil no longer than waist length and a short train or go ahead and wear formal attire even though your guest list is a bit small.

Q   I have not yet chosen my wedding dress, but my husband-to-be keeps insisting that he will not wear a "monkey suit." Does this mean I cannot wear a long dress with a veil?

A   Once you decide how formal your wedding will be, then everyone in the wedding party must dress accordingly. For a formal wedding, men wear white tie or "tails" during the evening and a black or gray sack coat during the daytime. This is, I assume, the outfit your future husband objects to wearing. For a semiformal wedding, the men wear black tie. (For more details on this dress, see chapter 5, "Entertaining and Being Entertained.") At an informal evening or daytime wedding, the groom wears a conservatively cut dark suit or, in the summer, dark trousers with a white linen jacket.

Now, what all this means is that you cannot go down the aisle in a formal wedding gown with a long train and veil if your groom is wearing a business suit. But there is room for compromise, if your groom will wear black tie. Then you can dress as formally as you like.

Q   I just got engaged, and I'm wondering how much time I will need to plan a wedding. I work full-time.

A   An informal wedding can be pulled together in two to three weeks, if the wedding goddess cooperates. A formal wedding requires a *minimum* of three to four months, and often longer—

not least because the reception rooms for such weddings are often booked as much as a year in advance.

If you can't take off much time from work, I suggest that you use the services of a wedding consultant. He or she can do much of the legwork for you and save you an enormous amount of time.

Q I am preparing my wedding invitation but am unsure of the proper wording.

A A formal wedding invitation reads:

Mr. and Mrs. James Smyley
request the honour of your presence
at the marriage of their daughter
Maria Louisa
to
Mr. Henry Woodstock
on Saturday, the first of August
at four o'clock
First Presbyterian Church
120 East Street
Cleveland, Ohio

Note the spelling of *honour*. The phrase *the honour of your presence* is used for a wedding held in a church or synagogue sanctuary or chapel. When the wedding takes place elsewhere, the wording is changed to *the pleasure of your company*.

Needless to say, there are many twists on invitations today—women are doctors, women who are doctors are marrying doctors, both sets of parents are included in the invitations, parents are divorced, etc. Should you need more detailed information, I suggest you consult my book *Your Complete Wedding Planner* (St. Martin's Press, 1989).

Q We want to include both sets of parents on the wedding invitation. Is this okay?

A It is not only okay, but I applaud this growing custom of .including both sets of parents.

Q I am a widow and am unable to make a financial contribution to my son's wedding. He just showed me the wedding announcements for the newspapers, and there is no mention of me. The bride's mother said that since I had not contributed anything, I could not be mentioned. Do you know anything about this?

A I know rude people when I encounter them. For one thing, the groom's family is under no obligation to help pay for the wedding. For another, as a matter of record, most newspapers will be interested in knowing who you are.

I suggest that you call the mother of the bride and express your wishes that you be included in the wedding notice. If she gives you any trouble, point out that you are making a very big contribution to the wedding: the groom.

Q I know I am going to have to struggle to keep the guest list down at my wedding. My parents have given me a budget, which I intend to abide by, but my future mother-in-law seems to think we can invite the world. Help!

A A wedding guest list is usually a struggle. If you cross this hurdle, planning the rest of your wedding is easy. I admire your consideration of your parents. Keep in mind that any wedding guest list is really made up of four lists: yours, your groom's, your parents', and his parents'. All must be merged, if not necessarily to everyone's immediate satisfaction. The usual precedence for invited guests is both your immediate families, your larger family circle, your friends, your parents' friends, and business associates or acquaintances of you and your parents. Knowing this, you will still have to juggle things. If the wedding is small, for example, the guest list may consist of only your immediate families and a few close friends. Remember that a wedding should not be used to pay back social obligations, so business associates and acquaintances can often be cut from a list that needs to be reduced.

Q Because of space and money limitations, we are not able to invite any small children to our wedding. How do I let people know this?

A You are wise to realize that you may have to take some extra steps. Obviously you can't print *No children, please* on the invitations, and some people may assume their children are invited, even though they aren't, unless their names are on the invitations. I suggest enclosing a personal, handwritten note to persons whom you think will be likely offenders. Explain that while you would love to include the children, it simply isn't possible.

Now believe it or not, you may still have to stand your ground through a few telephone calls from parents who have trouble taking no for an answer. Just keep repeating, "Really, we would love to have them, but we just can't make an exception for your children without hurting other people's feelings" And it's true. If you rule that no children are permitted, then don't make exceptions, or you will have hurt feelings among those whose children were excluded.

Q We want a great party more than a traditional wedding. Any suggestions?

A I hear this a lot these days and, yes, I can make some suggestions, although I think the best, most successful, weddings are those that combine a few avant-garde touches with traditional ones. Here are my suggestions:

- Wear a traditional dress with a funky touch, such as a touch of color, an interesting hemline, or a spectacular neckline (which you can cover up during the wedding and reveal during the reception).

- Order an unusual cake, perhaps one with real flowers or something nontraditional on top (a popular choice is a couple doing something they both love, be it skiing or sailing). The cake type can also be unusual: chocolate, carrot, poppy seed, or whatever pleases your palate.
- Choose unusual music. One bride I knew went down the aisle to the sixties rock song "Goin' to the Chapel." Needless to say, this wedding was not held in a church. The reception is where you can really cut loose with the music of your choice. A word of caution, though: Don't blast your guests with nonstop rock music during the reception unless everyone is your age, which is unlikely.
- Arrive at the church or temple in some unusual conveyance. At one wedding, the bride and groom arrived in a fire truck; it was appropriate since he was a fireman. Think about an antique car, a horse-drawn carriage, or a sled in winter.
- If you really want to go all out and have a lot of fun, plan a period wedding. Imagine what era you would most like to have lived in—Victorian, Edwardian, the Twenties, or even the Fifties—and dress yourselves and your wedding party accordingly.
- Tell the florist to forget it's a wedding when he plans your flowers. Go for drama or a period mood instead.

Q May I rent my wedding dress?
A Yes, and it's a very good idea since you will probably never wear it again. Keep in mind that no one need know, unless you want them to, that you have rented the dress.

Q My mother wants to wear a long dress to my wedding even though it will be at 2 P.M. I thought long dresses could not be worn before 6 P.M.

A Your mother is officially part of the wedding party, so she must dress with the same degree of formality that it does. This means that a long dress is appropriate at 2 P.M. if the wedding is very formal or semiformal. The mother of the bride also doesn't wear white or black.

Q As a guest, what do I wear to a 5 o'clock wedding?
A What you as a guest wear to a wedding depends upon the time of the wedding and, to some degree, its formality. A five o'clock wedding is a daytime wedding. Evening clothes are not worn before 6 P.M. At a formal or semiformal daytime wedding, female guests wear street-length clothes—dressy suits or silk dresses, for example. For a formal evening wedding, female guests wear either long or short evening dresses. For a semiformal evening wedding, female guests wear cocktail dresses. At an informal wedding, women guests wear suits or pretty dresses. Only at a formal evening wedding do the male guests wear tuxedos, and even then they are optional; at other times, males wear dark suits in the winter or, in the summer, light suits or navy blazers and light-colored pants.

Q How many attendants may I have at my wedding, and must I ask someone from the groom's family? He doesn't have a sister, but his brother is married.
A The number of attendants you have depends upon how formal your wedding is. At formal weddings, where as many as three or four hundred guests may have been invited, the bride may be attended by five or six women plus a junior bridesmaid and a flower girl. The groom may ask even more of his friends to attend him, since one usher is needed for every fifty guests. At the altar, though, the number of groomsmen always matches the number of female attendants.

As a courtesy, the bride asks the groom's sister, if he has one, to attend her, and he asks her brother to attend him. If the bride and groom do not have siblings, no other relative need be invited unless, of course, you want to.

Q I would ask my husband-to-be's sister to be a bridesmaid, but she is pregnant, and I don't want a pregnant attendant because of the difficulty in dressing her like everyone else in the wedding party. What is right here?

A Although I've seen pregnant attendants at a few weddings, it is still up to each individual bride whether or not she would like one. You're off the hook if you want to be. I do hope you will say something to her if you don't ask her. Let her know that you would have loved to have her as an attendant were she not pregnant.

Q My groom's sister has a three-year-old who is darling. Is she old enough to be my flower girl?

A Little girls are not generally trusted with the role of flower girl until they are four or five, but if your niece-to-be is an especially poised three-year-old, you might risk it. Understand that one of two things may happen: She may refuse to perform at the last minute, or she may steal the show. If you do make her your flower girl, I suggest that she walk in the processional only and skip the recessional. Have her join her mother right before reaching the altar. It is too much to ask a three-year-old to stand quietly throughout a wedding ceremony.

Q Can I ask a divorced woman to be my honor attendant? If so, is she a maid or matron of honor?

A Assuming that your clergyperson has no objections, you may ask someone divorced to stand up for you. If your friend is very recently divorced, you may want to sound her out to see if she feels like participating in a wedding at this point in her life, and while one does not decline an invitation to be a wedding attendant if one can possibly avoid it, I think it would be kind to let her tell you honestly if she will have any emotional difficulties with this.

She is your maid of honor since she is not married.

Q My best friend is a man, and I'm wondering if he can be my maid of honor. I know it's unusual, but I'm not having a very traditional wedding.

A Well, yes, he could be, I suppose, but I have another suggestion. Why not ask your husband-to-be if he will invite your friend to be one of his attendants? If you do decide to make a man your maid of honor, he still dresses like the other male attendants.

Q What instructions should I give our ushers about seating guests?

A Tell them the following:

- They should approach guests as they enter the sanctuary.
- If you are seating the bride's people on the left and the groom's people on the right, the usher should ask, "Are you a friend of the bride or the groom?"
- Ushers may also be instructed, if you wish, to balance out the church or even to seat people without regard to family ties.
- The usher should offer his arm to the first or most elderly of a group of women, to any gentleman who is elderly and infirm, and to any teen-age girls, who will be thrilled to be escorted down the aisle by him. Traditionally, he has also offered his arm to married or escorted women, but a newer way to handle this is for the usher to precede the couple down the aisle, letting the woman take her husband or escort's arm.

Q My mother, who is bedridden, is not well enough to attend my wedding, although she has helped me plan it. May I ask someone to stand in for her? I don't want to offend her or usurp her role in any way.

A Why don't you ask an aunt, sister, or family friend to watch over things in much the same way your mother would on your wedding day? That person should not stand in the receiving line; your father should do this.

Perhaps you can do something special to make your mother feel part of the wedding day. You could visit her as soon as possible after your reception to sit with her and watch a videotape of the wedding and reception. Be sure to send her a corsage to wear on your special day.

Q I know my divorced parents will not want to sit together at my wedding, even though neither one has remarried. What can I do?

A Your mother sits in the first pew or row of seats. She should not sit alone. If she invites an escort, he will sit with her; otherwise, she may ask her brother or some other close relative or family friend to sit with her. Your father, with his escort or a sister or close family friend, sits one or two pews or rows behind your mother.

Q My sister recently separated from her husband after ten years of marriage. I like my brother-in-law and would not like to exclude him from the wedding, especially since his oldest daughter will be a junior bridesmaid. Help!

A Talk with your sister and express your feelings about having her husband present. Ask her to tell you honestly how she feels. If she has no problem having him there, I suggest you invite him to the wedding and the reception. If she has a problem, ask if she would mind if you invited him to the wedding but not the reception. He will understand, I'm sure, and if there is any doubt about it, talk with him, too, after you have talked to your sister.

Q I desperately want a wedding picture of me with both my parents, now divorced and remarried for many years. Can you think of any way I can finagle this? Don't they owe me this much?

A They probably do owe you this, but you must take their feelings into account. It won't be much of a picture if you are standing between two glowering people.

First, don't spring this on them *at* the wedding; ask them a week or so before if they would pose together with you. If they agree, take that picture, and then take two more—of you with each parent and his or her present spouse.

Q Must the groom's family give the rehearsal dinner? My groom's parents live at the opposite end of the country and have never even been to our state, let alone our town. They have offered, but my mother thinks we should just do it.

A First, they aren't obligated to give the rehearsal dinner, and if the groom's family never mentioned doing so, it would be impolite for the bride's family to suggest it. In this case, however, the groom's family is not only willing, but is obviously game, even though they won't be on their own social turf. Before declining their kind invitation, I would try to work something out.

Check out several restaurants and clubs, preferably in a price range you think suits their pocketbook. Present them with the information you have gathered, and when they have chosen the place, you and your mother can make the arrangements. Also arrange for everything to be billed to them.

Q Who arranges lodging for out-of-town wedding guests? What are my obligations to them?

A You may either make reservations or send your out-of-town guests information about hotels (a selection, please!) and let them make their own reservations. You are not obligated to pay for lodging for out-of-town guests. In fact, you are not obligated to do much of anything, but you should be aware of their needs and try to meet them. It is kind to meet people at the airport, if at all possible, for example.

Out-of-town guests are usually invited to the rehearsal dinner, and some other festivities may be planned for them.

When you greet them at the wedding, make a point of telling them how pleased and flattered you are that they have come to your wedding.

Q I want the most sophisticated wedding ever, so I'm writing to ask you one question. Can my bridesmaids wear black?

A Your bridesmaids may wear black—a color that was taboo at weddings until a few years ago—and if they do, you may rest assured that you will have one of the most—if not the most—sophisticated weddings ever.

10

. . . .

PERSONAL LOSS

· Loss of a Loved One ·

Q My husband is terminally ill, and while I probably should not be thinking about practical matters, I have never lost anyone close to me, and I am not sure what to do when the moment of death comes.

A You are right to worry about practical matters. They, along with emotional concerns, must be dealt with when someone dies. Three things must be done immediately:

1. Call close relatives and friends.
2. Call your clergyperson and/or a funeral director. (Your clergyperson is usually called first because he or she will be able to suggest a funeral director to you. If you do not have a clergyperson to call, ask the hospital if you can talk with the clergyperson who is on call, who will be able to help you make the initial calls.)
3. Call the attorney of the deceased person, who will begin to probate his or her will.

These days, the telephone is usually used to notify family and friends of a death. If it is not possible to reach someone by telephone (they live in a remote village halfway around the world) or you do not reach them right away, a day letter, which is less expensive than a telegram, may be sent.

Q How do I arrange for a funeral notice for a member of my family?

A The funeral director will obtain the necessary information from you and arrange for death notices to be placed in your local papers as well as in newspapers in communities where the deceased was known or lived and might still have contacts. You must give him or her the following information:

- Name, including a woman's maiden name
- Date of death
- Names of survivors—usually spouses, parents, children, and siblings
- When and where the wake, if any, will be held
- When and where the funeral (or memorial service) will be held

Q When my husband died, the funeral director said he would notify the papers. He did, but all they printed was a short paragraph under the "Death Notices" section. My husband was a prominent educator, and I expected a longer write-up about him. Don't you think the funeral director should have been more aware of my husband's status?

A The funeral director did as he promised and took care of the death notices. A death notice, which is paid for, differs from an obituary, which is a newspaper article about a deceased person, usually someone prominent.

Newspapers decide when they will write obituaries, and there is little you can do to ensure that a departed loved one will be the recipient of one. I say "little," because it may help to have a family member—not the funeral director—call the newspaper directly to tell them that "Dr. Jones, who developed the theory of vertical education, died today." Similarly, you may have a slightly expanded typewritten death notice delivered to a newspaper in hopes that they will realize an obituary is in order. (Do not attempt to write the obituary yourself; merely supply the necessary information.) Finally, you can, as many others have done, some successfully and some not, use personal contacts—persons you know who are affiliated with a newspaper who may be able to help obtain an obituary.

Q   Must a cause of death be listed in the newspaper announcement? Our son is dying of AIDS, but we don't want to put this in the announcement.
A   There is no obligation—legal or social—to include a cause of death in a death announcement. The newspaper notice usually indicates that a person died "suddenly," which means unexpectedly, or "after a long illness." Of course, newspaper notices also give more detailed causes, indicating, for example, that the person died "after a long battle" with lung cancer or heart disease, and these days, far too often we hear of death due to AIDS.

I must add that there is considerable debate in some circles about the advisability of disguising a cause of death, particularly when the death was due to AIDS and knowledge of this fact might help others. To the extent that knowledge about a cause of death is denied, we all collude with the false notion that some deaths are shameful. Unless the cause of death is widely known, I usually advise people to include one in the death notices—if only to forestall awkward questions and rumors.

Q   What does one do upon learning of the news that a close friend has died?
A   The immediate family begins to gather as soon as they learn the sad news. They usually go directly to the home of the de-

ceased's spouse, children, or parents, whomever they are closest to. Other relatives and friends who are not chief mourners should do what they can to support those who are—the wife or husband, children, and parents of the person who died. They may call at the home, or telephone, in both cases offering their condolences and asking if they can be of any assistance.

Q I am writing my will and would like to make provisions for my pallbearers now. I hate to be spiteful, but there are some persons I don't want near me—even after I'm gone. How do I go about this?
A If you wish to leave instructions regarding your funeral, write them into a letter and tell one or more persons where they can find the letter when the time comes. Whatever you do, don't write invitations to your pallbearers into your will, because it quite likely will not be read until after you are buried. And do not put the letter in a lockbox, because your family may not have immediate access to it after you die.

If you wish, you can avoid choosing pallbearers and let the funeral director supply professional ones. These days, more often than not, professional pallbearers carry the casket out of the funeral home or church and at the cemetery. In any event, members of the immediate family never serve as pallbearers since they are too bereaved.

Pallbearers may be either honorary (nonworking) or actual. For a church or synagogue funeral, pallbearers are always honorary. A row is reserved for them so they can sit together at the front of the church or synagogue, usually directly behind the family. In any event, pallbearers, who are usually (but need not be) men, are chosen from among family and friends. Both Jews and Christians have pallbearers.

Q At what age should a child be permitted to attend a funeral?
A This depends upon the child. Children only come slowly to a realization of what death means, and this knowledge

should never be forced on them. Neither should a child who is mature enough to handle the experience be denied a chance to say good-bye to a loved one. I don't think children under the age of five can comprehend what a funeral is all about, nor can they be counted on to sit through a service. After five, I think children can be permitted to attend funerals if they want to—and if the person is someone with whom they were especially close.

Q May I attend the funeral of my ex-husband? We have been divorced for eighteen years. He has since remarried and has another family. I certainly don't want to embarrass anyone.
A Use your discretion and best judgment, but I see no reason why you should not attend the funeral. Your presence, however, should be a low-key one. Don't expect to sit with the family, and unless everyone at the funeral is going to the cemetery, I would not recommend making this trip. I do have a suggestion that may make things easier for you: Take a good friend along for moral support and comfort.

Q My ex-husband's aunt died, and although I have not seen her in the five years that I have been divorced, she was once a very special person to me. May I attend her funeral?
A You may, but I suggest that you make your presence as unobtrusive as possible. You may call at the funeral home, too, and express your condolences to the family.

Q My husband's father has a terminal illness and will not live long. He never approved of our marriage and has rarely even spoken to me in the fifteen years I have been married. Fortunately for family relations, he lives 3,000 miles away. Must I attend his funeral? I find that I am very bitter at the prospect of doing so. My husband says he understands and will not object if I do not come with him.

A I can understand your bitterness, and I have known other persons in your very sad situation. In a sense, I think you are off the hook if you want to be because of the distance involved. If you do not travel the 3,000 miles for the funeral, it will seem a little odd, but most persons will understand. But this is also a time to think of your husband, your children, if you have any, and your other in-laws. Will they need your moral support for the day? Will your absence be another major loss to them? Sometimes we must rise above our own pain to do something that will relieve another's.

Q My children, aged eight and five, will be expected to attend the funeral of their paternal grandmother, who is very ill. The children's father and I have been divorced for less than a year, our feelings toward one another are very bitter, and everyone in our families has taken sides. I would like to say my children cannot attend this funeral; failing that, I would like to be there with them since this is their first experience with death, even though this will upset my husband's family. Is this a reasonable request?

A Swallow your pride and, for the sake of your children, talk to your former husband. The two of you should decide together whether the children should attend this funeral. And you may be surprised at his views on this.

If you do decide they should attend, or if it becomes obvious to you that their presence will be very important to your ex-husband, then let him handle the situation. Your presence would, as you have admitted, further upset his family at a time when they are entitled to be treated with special care. Don't forget that you can talk with your children before and after the funeral to help them comprehend what is happening.

Q My daughter recently committed suicide. I have two questions: Must I tell people she died this way, and was I wrong not to honor her wish to be cremated? Cremation is against our religion, and I couldn't bring myself to do it.

A I believe the survivors need not always honor the last wishes of the dead; if you preferred to bury your daughter, it was right to do so. The rituals surrounding death are, I believe, for the living.

As for the way your daughter died, no, you need not tell anyone. But wouldn't it be easier on you to talk to a few people—perhaps someone professional—about what has happened? As we have broadened our understanding of mental illness, the stigma attached to suicide has lessened considerably, and you do not have to carry this heavy burden by yourself or treat it as a deep, dark family secret. Others will be sympathetic and supportive.

Q What should I do when I learn that a good friend has lost her husband? Last year this happened to a friend, and I simply went to the funeral. My friend was furious with me for "not doing more." But I've lost very few people in my life and wasn't sure what "more" was. I called her a few days after the funeral and have made special efforts to see her ever since. What more could I do?

A I think your friend may have been referring to the hours and days between the death and funeral. Very close friends usually go to the house of the bereaved as soon as they learn of the death. They offer their assistance—and are often put to work calling relatives, making funeral arrangements, buying clothes for the funeral, driving family members, attending to small children, and so on. Close friends also usually bring in food for the family to eat for the few days of their initial bereavement.

Q My wife wants to be cremated, and we have discussed her funeral plans. We aren't sure what kind of service should be planned, though. Can you help us?

A A funeral is held for someone who will be cremated. The family may accompany the deceased's body to the crematorium if they wish but, more often, the clergyperson incorporates the graveside prayers into the funeral service, and the family does not go to the cemetery. If the person has already been cremated, there is no funeral, but instead a memorial service may be held.

Q How does one go about calling at the funeral home when a friend has died?

A Close friends and relatives, of course, will have gone to the bereaved's home, but they and others may also call at the funeral home before the funeral. The death notice will give the hours for calling and the address of the funeral home. (Note that this custom is followed only for Protestants and Catholics; Jews do not have a wake before the funeral.)

The hours listed in the death notice indicate when members of the family will be present. You need not call during those hours, however, and may in fact call at any time to sign the register. If you are a close friend, relative, or neighbor, though, you will want to make a special point of calling when the family is there so you can comfort them personally.

It is usual when you call at a funeral home to view the body. When doing so, you may follow your own customs. Only Roman Catholics kneel or cross themselves. Protestants usually stand for a moment with their heads bowed. If you prefer not to view the body, when asked to do so, simply say, "No, thank you. I want to remember Annette as she was."

Before or after you view the body, you will greet family members. Shake hands and tell them how sorry you are for their loss. If they seem inclined to talk, listen sympathetically. If they seem unable to handle conversation, move away discreetly.

Q If I call at the funeral home to sign the register, must I also attend the funeral? Must I also send a condolence note?

A   Whether or not you attend the funeral has nothing to do with whether you call at the funeral home, although persons who know they cannot attend a funeral usually make a special effort to call at the funeral home.

If you sign the register and do not greet the family, you should still send a personal note of condolence. If you offer your condolences personally, a note is not needed.

Q   What are the right words of condolence to say to someone who has lost someone he loved?
A   Three very simple words will do: "I'm so sorry." Apart from this, there are no right words. You need not say much or be eloquent to offer comfort to someone who has suffered the loss of a loved one. Just be there for them in their time of loss. If you can recall a particularly pleasant or interesting time you spent with the deceased, and the mourners seem inclined to hear about it, you might talk about this.

Those in mourning do discuss things other than the loss of their loved one, so don't be surprised—or horrified—if the weather comes up. People have a way of taking care of their needs at such times.

Q   I would like to have a church funeral, but I have never attended one. What is the procedure and ritual?
A   Contact your clergyperson to make arrangements with him or her. A church funeral always feels more like a church service to me, but I think this is only because I'm in church. Regardless of whether your funeral is at a church or a funeral home, the service will be the same, with prayers and hymns in addition to the eulogy.

Q   I've been invited to a church funeral. What do I do?
A   Church funerals are so rare these days that most people think some special behavior is expected of them even though it

isn't. Whether the funeral is held in a church or funeral home, arrive about fifteen minutes early. Sit up front if you are a family member or a close friend. Enter quietly. The immediate family usually enters after everyone has arrived, often through a private entrance, and they may leave first. They need not stop to talk to people, although one family member may be designated to quietly greet those who have come.

After the funeral, the family proceeds immediately to the cemetery for the graveside service. For Protestants and Roman Catholics, only the immediate family and a few close friends go. As many people as are able go to the cemetery for a Jewish funeral.

Q I'm a Protestant married to a Jewish woman. Unfortunately, one of these days I will have to attend a funeral in her family. Can you prepare me for what to expect and what is expected of me?
A The Jewish religion requires that burial be held as soon as possible after death, although it cannot be held on the Sabbath (from sundown Friday to sundown Saturday) or during a major holiday. There is no prefuneral visiting, either at the funeral home or at the home of the bereaved, although you may, if asked, visit with the bereaved to help them make funeral plans.

Jewish funerals are rarely held in a synagogue. The coffin, which is plain, is closed permanently before the funeral. Family members may have private viewing prior to the funeral if they wish. The service is usually short, although if the person is prominent, it may be longer, as many people will eulogize the deceased.

As was noted in the preceding question, everyone who can goes with the family to the cemetery for the graveside service. In the Conservative and Orthodox denominations, a minimum of thirteen men are necessary to say *kaddish,* a mourners' prayer; Reform Judaism permits the family and friends to say it. By tradition, the family usually stays until the grave is covered; often, friends stay with them and may even assist in covering the coffin. Another tradition is for those attending the grave-side service to form two lines for the chief mourners to walk through when they leave the grave site.

The family and friends gather at the home of the deceased or a close relative immediately after the funeral and begin sitting *shivah,* a three- to seven-day mourning period during which the bereaved stay home, do not follow ordinary pursuits, and receive visitors. A pitcher of water and a towel may be placed outside the door at a Jewish home after a funeral; guests dip their hands into the water and dry them before entering the house.

Q A friend who is Jewish lost her husband recently. I was told there would be no wake, so I attended the funeral. I felt I did very little to comfort my friend. What else could I have done?
A You could have called on your friend while she was sitting *shivah.* While Jews do not accept calls in the period between the death and the funeral, they do welcome calls from friends and relatives in the days following the funeral. The hours when the family is receiving callers are usually listed in the death announcement in the newspaper and at the funeral.

Q I would prefer to have a memorial service when I die. What kind of arrangements should be made for this?
A A memorial service is very much like a funeral, except there is no body. A clergyperson usually officiates, and prayers are said for the deceased.

If the memorial service is held soon after the death, flowers may be sent, as they would be for a funeral.

If the memorial service is held several months after the death, flowers are not sent by family and friends, although bouquets are usually ordered for the altar or dais.

The clergyperson of the deceased may officiate, or the service may be ecumenical or even secular. Friends often speak briefly, sharing their memories of the deceased. When the deceased was prominent in the artistic or theatrical community, a poem or short passage from a favorite book may be read, or colleagues may perform in honor of the departed.

Q Who may attend a funeral or memorial service?

A Unless the obituary or death announcement states that the funeral or memorial service is private, either one may be attended by anyone who knew the person. When a funeral is private, invitations are usually issued by telephone, and a list of invitees is usually kept at the door. Persons who were not invited are not admitted.

One attends the funeral or memorial service of any close relative or friend, as well as certain acquaintances. Whether or not you attend the funeral or memorial service of a business associate or other acquaintance depends upon your personal feelings toward the person and his or her family. You need not know the family to attend the service. Even strangers offer comfort, and people need the solace of one another at such times; it is better to attend a service when you aren't sure whether you should go than not to attend and be missed—or have regrets later on.

Q What is the right attire for a funeral?

A While black is still worn by mourners, it is no longer required, and widows need not wear black after the funeral—or even at the funeral, if they don't choose to. A widow may even choose, for example, to wear a dress that her husband particularly liked—regardless of its color. If the dress is red or some other gay color, she may want to mention her reason for wearing it to those attending the service, lest they get the wrong impression. Men wear conservative dark suits and ties; most sports jackets are inappropriate at a funeral. Children never wear black for mourning; they wear their best clothes of whatever color, or they wear white. White is also worn in the tropics for mourning.

As a general guideline, anyone attending a funeral should choose something somber over something brightly colored to wear.

Q   Are funerals held for babies who are stillborn? A couple I know lost a baby this way, and they held a funeral service. I had never heard of such a thing.
A   Couples used to be discouraged, as part of the healing process, from holding any kind of service for a stillborn infant, the feeling being that they should put this unpleasant experience behind them as soon as possible.

Today, thank goodness, we have become much more sensitive to people's needs regarding loss, including the loss of a stillborn infant. We understand that people need room to mourn such losses and that the mourning process may involve some kind of ceremony, if this will help to console the parents.

Such services are small, attended only by the parents, and perhaps a few other family members, and a few intimate friends. I recommend a memorial service, where there will be no casket. Friends and relatives usually don't send flowers, but it would be a special kindness to send flowers to the family in the weeks thereafter. The family may order flowers for the altar or podium.

Depending upon the family's religious affiliation and the age of the fetus, there may be restrictions on the type of service or burial that can be arranged. The family should check with their clergyperson before making any plans.

Q   My parents' anniversary, the first one since my father died, is next month. I know it will be a rough time for my mother, and I want to acknowledge it. Should I send an anniversary card anyway?

A   Skip the anniversary card, which is no longer suitable for the occasion, and send a letter instead so your mother will know you remembered. It would be a kind gesture to plan a quiet dinner with your mother. It is acceptable to toast your father's memory.

Q   Is it ever proper to send a printed sympathy card?
A   Not really, although I realize that card companies make and sell such cards. Death is the one occasion where a truly personal touch is called for, and I think this still means a handwritten note expressing your sympathies.

A sympathy note need not be long or even too specific. Simply say something like this: "I was so sorry to learn of your loss, and I want you to know that my thoughts are with you. If I can do anything, please let me know."

If you knew the deceased person well, you may want to write a slightly longer note or letter in which you recall a special moment spent with the deceased. His or her family will treasure the memory and be grateful to you for taking the time to share it with them.

Q   How long after a death may a condolence note be sent?
A   You may send a condolence note at any time that you hear about the death. It would be unusual but kind—and perfectly acceptable—to send a note a year or more after a death if that is when you learned about it. Most notes are sent within a week or so after the announcement of the death.

Q   When my mother died, more than 100 bouquets were sent to the funeral. The funeral director gave me some printed thank-you cards, but my daughter maintains it is improper to use them. She says I must sent handwritten notes of thanks. I would, but I have arthritis, and it will take me forever to write those notes.
A   Usually, the funeral director retrieves the cards attached to flowers and gives them to the family so they can respond. The

family must also thank people for any donations made on behalf of the deceased or any funeral masses that are offered. These days, he also supplies printed thank-you cards, which increasing numbers of people have begun to use. I still favor a handwritten thank-you note.

You need not write the notes yourself, though, and I suggest that you enlist the aid of your daughter and/or other relatives and close friends. The notes are written on behalf of the family.

If you must write them and know that you will need a long period of time in which to do so, or an overwhelming number of tributes were sent, the family may send printed cards that say:

> *The family of James Smith*
> *gratefully acknowledges*
> *receipt of your kind gift*
> *and will respond personally*
> *at the earliest opportunity.*

Notes should be written on white or off-white paper with a blue or black pen.

Q Can a condolence note ever be typed?
A You may send a typed condolence note to a business associate.

Q A very close friend died recently, and I was upset, not for the first time, to find that the family was requesting that a contribution be made to charity in lieu of flowers. I like the custom of sending flowers to a bereaved family. Could I have sent flowers anyway?
A It is a kindness to honor the family's wishes. Only the immediate family and very close friends may still send flowers to a

funeral when the family requests that none be sent. Some people feel funeral flowers are an unnecessary expense and that the money is better spent on some charitable cause. The contribution to charity, by the way, should equal the amount you would have spent on flowers. Finally, if you really feel a need to send flowers, how about sending a cheery bouquet or potted plant to the family a week or so after the funeral when they often can really use such a considerate gesture?

Q More and more funeral notices request that contributions be made to charities in lieu of flowers. How do I choose the charity, and how do I go about making sure the family knows about my gift?

A If a charity is not suggested in the death announcement, try to make a contribution to one that has some tie to a special interest of the deceased. If he or she loved children, for example, you might make a donation to a charity that works for children. Alternatively, you may make a contribution to the charity that supports research to eradicate the disease from which the deceased died.

Send a check and a note, telling the charity that this contribution is being made "in memory of John Smith." Usually, the charity then sends a note to the family, but to be sure they learn of your contribution, you should also send the family a note telling them of your donation. Naturally, the amount you donated is not mentioned.

Q How does one know when flowers will be acceptable at a funeral in these times when so many people are requesting that no flowers be sent?

A Unless the family requests that no flowers be sent in the death announcement, flowers may be sent to the funeral of any Protestant or Catholic. Flowers are not usually sent to a Reform Jewish funeral, and they are never sent to the funeral of a

Conservative or Orthodox Jew. When in doubt, contact the funeral home or the rabbi who will officiate at the funeral.

Flowers are sent to the funeral home and are addressed *To the funeral of John Smith.* If the clergyperson or the family so desires, they will be transferred to a church for the funeral service. Catholic churches, for example, allow only the flowers of the immediate family.

Q What happens after a funeral? Does the family just go home alone? I've heard about wakes but have never attended one.
A A formal wake, which refers to keeping watch over a body, is rarely held today. At a wake, friends and family traditionally congregate, and in the course of sharing memories and meals with one another (in some cultures), such occasions often became somewhat festive.

Today a wake typically consists of family and friends calling at the funeral home. After the burial, close relatives and friends also may gather, usually at the home of the deceased, for a meal and reminiscences. Food is brought to the family by friends or a church organization; they do not prepare a meal in the midst of their mourning.

Q My aunt invited me to attend an unveiling for my late uncle. I have another commitment that day but am wondering if the unveiling takes precedence.
A An unveiling, the Jewish ceremony held at the cemetery to unveil the headstone or monument, takes place one year after the deceased dies. It is an important family event, and you should probably arrange to attend if you possibly can. Family, and sometimes close friends, are invited to attend, and light refreshments are usually served at the grave site or at someone's home afterward.

Q I want to arrange a mass in memory of a deceased friend, but I am not Catholic. How do I go about doing this?

A Contact your friend's church or any Catholic church for that matter. Expect to make a donation. The church will send a card notifying the family that a mass will be said, but you should also send a note letting them know what you have done. You need not be Catholic to arrange for a mass in someone's behalf.

Q My husband recently died. What is expected of me as a mourner? May I go out socially? Must I wear black?
A Mourning today is a state of mind rather than a social condition. You may, but need not, wear black. As for going out, it is considered healthy to resume your normal activities as soon as you feel up to it—even within a week or so of the funeral.

· Death of a Pet ·

Q Our family has a dog, whom we all dearly love. My problem is this: The dog is old and will probably die soon. Would it be silly to have a service or funeral of some kind for the dog? I think it would help my children.
A People often mourn pets as much as they do a member of the family whom they have lost. And while it would be appropriate for you to arrange for some sort of ceremony, I would not make too much of it.

I suggest, for example, that only your family should be present. Prayers should be said by you and your children, not a clergyperson, assuming you could even get one to participate in such an event. (I have heard of stranger things, though.)

Attempts to elevate a funeral service for an animal to the level of that held for a person are demeaning to human life. This is not to say you and your children will not mourn the loss of your beloved pet, merely that your mourning will be more understated and private than it would be for a human member of your family.

· Separation and Divorce ·

Q My husband and I recently separated, but we are hoping to work things out. Need I tell my friends about this?

A A separation is not officially announced because, presumably, the persons involved are trying to work out issues and make a go of their marriage. You may, of course, discuss your separation with close friends, but unless you bring it up, others should not mention it.

Q How do I announce my recent divorce? It seems like dreary news for a Christmas card.

A A divorce may be dreary news for a Christmas card, but that is exactly where most people end up announcing it. I suspect it would be drearier still to sit down and write letters to all of one's friends just to announce a divorce. If you can't bear to mar your holiday message, you can let people find out via the grapevine. Most people, however, end up adding a short note to their Christmas cards that says: "I suppose you have heard the sad news that Bob and I divorced in June."

Q May I send printed announcements of my divorce? I am thinking that this would be a good way to inform acquaintances and friends whom I don't see very often, as well as my bank and other vendors.

A A divorce is never formally announced via printed cards or letters. Such announcements sound as if the parties involved are celebrating, an impression that must be avoided at all costs. You are under no obligation to announce your change in status to vendors and others with whom you have business dealings. Indeed, no explanation is necessary with acquaintances and business associates whom you do not see regularly.

There is a way you can announce your new single status. If

you moved to a new address, send change-of-address cards. When your ex-spouse's name is not on the card, people will get the message.

Q   I'm very unhappy over my divorce, and it was messy. Everyone wants to know the details, but so far I've kept them to myself. Must I be discreet about this? I truly feel my husband did me wrong, and I'd like the world to know about it.

A   Although I sympathize with how you feel, I still urge you to keep the details to yourself or to share them with only one or two very discreet friends, especially if you have children: They won't be helped by your smearing their father's reputation.

A more important reason to keep your own confidence, I feel, is that you will like yourself better. What good can come from constantly replaying an unhappy episode in your life? It's time to pick up the pieces and start all over. This, more than anything else, will help to erase the pain you are feeling.

Q   What is my name now that I am divorced? My mother insists that I be called Sally Mainline Ryan, with Mainline being our family name and Ryan being my ex-husband's name.

A   Divorcées used to adapt a combination of their maiden names and their married names (Sally Mainline Ryan, for example), but this is considered stuffy today, and most divorced women become simply Sally Ryan. Many resume the use of their maiden names and become Sally Mainline again. You can use either Miss or Mrs., the latter being preferred by women with children. What you cannot be any longer is Mrs. John Ryan, since that title will belong to your ex-husband's next wife, and too much confusion, of a kind you would not like, would result from that.

Q   Do I continue to wear a wedding ring even though I'm divorced? I do have children, so I think I should wear it for them.

A Until a decade or so ago, divorced women with children usually continued to wear their wedding rings. Most divorced women today no longer wear a wedding band, even if they have children. I recommend not wearing one, for your sake. It's time to get on with the rest of your life.

There is no social stigma attached to being a mother and not wearing a wedding ring these days. Single mothers do not wear them; divorced women, more often than not, do not; and even happily married mothers sometimes, for one reason or another, do not wear wedding bands.

Q Am I still related to my ex-in-laws even though I'm divorced? I'm still good friends with my sister-in-law. Can I introduce her this way?

A Sorry, but you are no longer related. Why not introduce her as your very good friend—she'll appreciate the warmth.

Q What is my relationship to my ex-in-laws? We had a rocky one at best when I was married, and I'm not too eager to maintain ties now that I no longer have a reason to do so.

A The relationship doesn't sound too hospitable. There is no real reason to maintain it, unless you have children. If you do have children, I urge you to maintain some ties with your ex-in-laws because not doing so will deprive your children of something very special—grandparents who can provide them with extra support and love at a time when they may badly need it.

Q I recently bumped into an old acquaintance and was shocked to learn that she and her husband had divorced. I didn't know what to say to her. What is appropriate in such circumstances?

A Say "I'm sorry" and don't pry. If you have enjoyed her company in the past, you might make an effort to include her in some activities now that she is probably in the process of reorganizing her social life.

Q I recently learned of a friend's divorce. Although she was my original friend (we went to college together), I always found her husband very attractive and would be interested in pursuing my friendship with him. Can I call him?

A Unfortunately, friends do choose sides in a divorce, but I suspect you have something else in mind. If you truly have become better friends with your friend's husband than with her over the years, I could see your favoring him over her, but you seem to be drawn to him only for his potential as an escort. And you seem to be showing no sympathy or consideration for your friend.

I suggest that you not call her husband. If he calls you, that is another matter.

Q My husband and I recently separated, and our divorce will probably be a long, drawn-out process. When can I start dating again?

A So long as you are trying to work out your marriage, it would not be appropriate to see other men. If the separation is definitely a prelude to a divorce, then you may begin dating—discreetly—whenever you feel up to it.

I say "discreetly" because a woman who is separated is still—legally and socially—a married woman. It would be appropriate for you to spend a quiet evening with a man—perhaps having dinner and going to a movie—but it would not be appropriate for you to take him to a friend's wedding, to an office party, or even home to your parents just yet. These same guidelines apply, of course, to men.

11

. . . .

TIPPING

MOST PEOPLE, at one time or another, experience some confusion over tipping, worrying either that they're tipping too little or too much. I've enclosed this tipping chart to help you know who, when, and how much to tip.

· *Tipping Chart* ·

PERSON	SERVICE	AMOUNT
Maitre d'hotel	Checks your reservation and shows you to your table	No tip unless special service is performed; then $3 to $5

PERSON	SERVICE	AMOUNT
Captain	Takes drink order, explains dishes on menu, recommends dishes, carves, flambées, or otherwise prepares food at table	5 percent of total bill
Waiter/room-service waiter in hotel	Serves food	15 percent of total bill
Lunch counter server	Serves food, beverage	10 percent, minimum 50 cents
Bartender	Serves drinks at bar	15 percent, minimum 50 cents
Strolling musician	Plays requests	Nothing, unless special request is made; $1 per request
Restroom attendant		Minimum 50 cents
Checkroom attendant	Checks coats	Never less than $1 for one coat; $1 for two coats; $2 and up for more than two coats

PERSON	SERVICE	AMOUNT
Doorman	Opens door	No tip
	Parks car	50 cents
	Hails cab	50 cents
	Hails cab in bad weather	$1
Taxi driver		Rarely is less than 50 cents given as tip for short rides; for longer rides, tip 10 to 15 percent
Skycap	Handles bags in airport	$1 per bag, more for large trunks
Redcap	Handles bags in train stations	May have set fee of $1 to $1.25 per bag; if not, tip this amount, more for large trunks
Chambermaid	Cleans room in hotel or motel	$2 per night for two persons; add $1 for each additional person
Bellman	Carries bags to hotel room, checks out room for you	$1 per bag, more for large trunk or many shopping bags

PERSON	SERVICE	AMOUNT
Barber		$1 to $2 per service in a small town; 15 percent of total bill in a city
Hairdresser or anyone else who provides service in beauty salon		15 percent of bill, divided among those who served you; $1 to $3 to shampoo person, depending upon service provided; tip owner nothing but give gift at Christmas
Shoeshine	Shoes Boots	50 cents $1
Movers	For major move of entire household	$5 per person per hour in cities; $5 to $10 per person in small towns
Mail person	Delivers mail and packages	$5 to $10 at Christmas
Newspaper delivery person		$5 to $15 at Christmas, depending upon service

PERSON	SERVICE	AMOUNT
Delivery person (groceries, drugs, furniture)		$1 to $2 for small deliveries $2 to $10 for large deliveries
Household help	Childcare, regular cleaning, gardening, or yard work	Tip one week's salary at Christmas; $5 to $15 for extra service throughout year
Apartment-building staff	Elevator operators	$10 to $15
	Porters	$10 to $15
	Doormen	$20 to $25
	Superintendent	$50; or tip less and give tips throughout year for special services
Caterer	Provides food	No tip, but tip service staff 15 percent of bill

Finally, I'd like to leave you with a list of persons who should never be tipped because to do so would be insulting. You may, however, buy them a present if they have extended some extraordinary service or done you a special favor:

- Secretary or office support staff (Cleaning person excepted; he or she will appreciate a tip from you.)

- Clergyperson (Strictly speaking, they are not "tipped," even though you may give a clergyperson a gift of money for services rendered such as a wedding or christening. What this really means is that you never remark that you tipped a clergyman such-and-such an amount.)
- Physicians, nurses, and other health workers (They are professionals and should be given presents, not money.)
- Shop owners (Don't tip the owner of a beauty shop, for example, but rather, give him or her a present.)
- Your children (A tip is different from an allowance, and both you and your children should understand the difference.)
- Your friends and relatives (Never, ever, no matter how much someone does for you, offer a friend or relative a tip; always give him or her a present—of considerable value if the occasion calls for it—for any special favors.)

·INDEX·

Address change, announcing, 77–78
Address labels, using, 80
Affection, displaying in public, 19
Age and friendship, 11
A la carte menu, 47
Anniversary celebrations, 55, 70–71, 85–87, 112–114
 after death of one spouse, 152–153
Announcements
 death, 141–142
 divorce, 158
 graduation, 112
 wedding, 131
Answering machines, 97–98

Applause, 45
Arguments at dinner party, 10
Attendants (wedding), 134–136, 139
Audience, being polite in, 44–46

Bar Mitzvah, 107–108
Bathrooms, public, 53–54
Birthdays, 108–110
Black tie, 56, 129
Blind people, helping, 27
Boss, getting along with, 28–29
Bridesmaids, 134–136, 139
Bris (naming ceremony), 104–106

Broken engagements, 118–119
Business cards, using, 42
Business correspondence, 42–43
Business life, 28–43
Business lunch, 28–29, 36–40

Calling cards, 80
Candles at the table, 65
Cards, sending, 90–93
Catholic ceremonies, 104,
    106–107, 156–157
Champagne
  at christening, 102
  glasses for, 65
Chanukah cards, 92–93
Children
  addressing adults, 13–14
  adult friends and, 10
  answering the phone, 94
  birthdays and, 108–110
  community and, 21–23
  funerals and, 143–145,
    151–152
  invitations and, 11–12, 23,
    55, 87, 132
  thank-you notes and, 89,
    110
  titles and, 81
Christening, 101–104
Christmas
  cards, 91–93
  gifts, 3–5, 72–76
  visiting family, 6–8
Church. See Religious services

City life, being a neighbor,
    20–21
Clients, getting along with,
    40–42
Cocktail hour, 67–68
Colleagues, business, 30–36
Community life, 20–27
Condolence notes, 41–42, 148,
    153–154
Confirmations, 72, 107–108
Congratulation letters, 90
Contributions to charity and
    funerals, 154–155
Correspondence
  business, 42–43
  general, 77–82
Coughing at a performance,
    45
Co-workers, getting along with,
    30–36
Cremation, 146–147

Dating
  bringing dates to parties, 29
  gifts and, 73–74
  introducing dates, 19
  while separated, 161
Deaf people, talking with, 27
Death, 140–157
Declining invitations, 8, 55–57,
    124
Delivery people, tipping, 23–24.
    See also Tipping.
Diets, 37–38, 68

Dinner party, 61
    arguments at, 10
    family obligations and, 3
    gifts, bringing to, 62–63
    seating arrangements, 67
    tardiness to, 59
Disabled people, 26–27
Divorce and separation,
    158–161
Divorced family and friends, 14,
    124–125, 135–138,
    144–145
Doggy bags, 50
Drinks when invited out, 39,
    47, 68

Eating out, 46–50. *See also*
    Business lunch
Elbows on the table, 69
Engagements (marriage),
    115–119
Entertaining and being
    entertained, 55–69
    for business, 36–41
Exchanging gifts at the store,
    75–76, 123

Family relationships, 1–8
    engagements and, 115–119
Feuds and invitations, 1
Fired friends at work,
    supporting, 33–34
First Communion, 106–107

First names vs. last names,
    13–15, 29, 42–43
Flatware, setting and using,
    64–67
Flower girls (weddings), 135
Flowers, sending, 74
    and funerals, 154–156
    and promotions, 74
Formal dress. *See* White tie
Friendships, 8–13, 17–18
    and bereavement, 146
    at work, 30, 35–36
Funeral homes, 147–148
Funeral notices, 141–142
Funerals, 143–157
Fur coats, when to wear, 36

Gallantry, 18–19, 34–35
Gay couples, 31
Getting acquainted in the
    community, 20–21
Gifts, giving and receiving,
    70–76
    for babies, 102, 105–106
    from family, 3–5
    graduation and, 112
    weddings and, 75–76,
        121–124
Godparents, choosing, 102–103
Graduation, 79–80, 111–112
Guest, being a, 58, 60–64
    visiting family on holidays,
        6–8
Guest of honor, 63

Holidays
  cards, 91–93
  gifts, 3–5, 72–76
  visiting family, 6–8
Host/Hostess, being a, 57–60
Housekeeper answering the
    phone, 93–94

Informal notes, 78–79, 85–86
In-laws, 2–4, 14, 160
Introductions, 13–17
  dates and, 19
  first names vs. last names,
    13
  living together and, 19
  step relatives and, 1–2
Invitations, 82–87
  children and, 10–12, 23, 55,
    132
  christening and, 103
  date, bringing a, 29
  declining, 8, 55–57, 124
  family feuds and, 1
  family obligations and, 3
  initiating friendships and, 8,
    17–18
  parties and, 55–57
  phone and, 96
  showers and, 99–100,
    119–120
  uninvited guests and, 25–26,
    60
  wedding and, 30, 82–85, 87,
    130–132

Jewish ceremonies, 104–108,
    110, 149–150, 156
Jokes in bad taste, reacting to, 3

"Ladies first?" 18
Last-minute invitations, 57
Last names vs. first names,
    13–15, 29, 42–43
Lateness, 44, 60
Letters. See Correspondence
Living together
  introducing your partner, 19
  sleeping arrangements when
    visiting parents, 5–6
Loss of a loved one, 140–157

Maiden name vs. married name,
    43, 80–81, 159
Male-female relations, 17–19
  at work, 34–36, 40–41
Married name vs. maiden name,
    43, 80–81, 159
Mass for the dead, 156–157
Memorial services, 150–151
Money as a gift, 72, 88, 114
Mourning, 151–152, 157
Moving, 20–21
  announcing new address,
    77–78

Names
  after divorce, 159

Names (*cont'd*)
  first vs. last, using, 13–15, 29, 42–43
  in-laws, what to call, 2–3
  mispronouncing, 16
  remembering, 16–17
  titles and, 80–81
Naming ceremonies, 104–106
Neighbors
  children of, 21–23
  dropping in on, 25–26, 60
  meeting, 20–21
  ongoing relations with, 25–27

Obituaries, 141–142

Pallbearers, 143
Parties, 10, 26, 30, 55–57, 108–114. *See also* Dinner party; Guest, being a; Host/Hostess, being a; Invitations
Passing food, 39–40, 48, 49, 66
Pet, death of a, 157
Place cards, using, 67
Plane travel, 51–52
Promotions, 31, 35–36, 74
Protestant ceremonies, 104, 107
Public courtesies, 44–46
Public life, 44–54

Questions (personal), topics to avoid, 9–10

Receiving gifts, 74–76
Receiving lines, 126–127
Rehearsal dinner (wedding), 138–139
Religious services, 52–53
  ceremonies, 101–108
  funerals and, 148
  mass for the dead, 156–157
Response cards (invitations), 83–85
Restaurants, eating at, 46–50. *See also* Business lunch

Salad, when to eat, 47–48
Sauce spoon, 69
Semi-formal dress. *See* Black tie
Separation and divorce, 158–161
Shiva, sitting, 150
Showers (parties), 99–101, 119–121
Signatures, 81
Silverware, setting and using, 64–67
Smoking, 46
Staff and service people, tipping, 23–25
Standing ovation, 44–45

Stationery (writing paper),
    78–80, 85–86
Step relatives, introducing, 1–2
Stillborn babies, funerals for,
    152
Strangers, talking to, 51, 54
Suicide, 145–146
Sympathy cards, 41–42, 148,
    153–154

Table d'hôte menu, 47
Table manners, 64–69
Tardiness, 44, 60
Telephone, using the, 93–98
Telephone answering machines,
    97–98
Telephone solicitation, 95
Thank-you notes, 3–4, 88–89,
    101, 110, 123, 153–154
Tipping, 23–25, 50–52, 162–167
Titles, 43, 80–81, 159
Train travel, 51–52
Travel, 51–52
Typing personal letters, 82, 90,
    154

Unveilings, 156
Ushers (wedding), 136

Visiting family on the holidays,
    6–8. *See also* Guest,
    being a

Wakes, 156
Wedding, 58–59, 121–139
    gifts, 75–76, 121–124
    invitations, 30, 82–85, 87,
        130–132
    seating at, 63–64
    thank-you notes, 89,
        123
Wedding consultant, 130
White tie, 56–57, 129
Wine, glasses for, 65
Wrong numbers (telephone),
    97

Your Complete Wedding Planner
    (Stewart), 130